HOW TO JUMPSTART A STALLED CAREER

Charles C. Prugh

VGM Career Horizons
a division of *NTC Publishing Group*
Lincolnwood, Illinois USA

Library of Congress Cataloging-in-Publication Data

Prugh, Charles C.
    How to jumpstart a stalled career / Charles C. Prugh.

        p.   cm.
    ISBN 0-8442-4171-7 (sft.)
    1. Career changes.   2. Career development.   I. Title.
HF5384.P78
650.14—dc20   93-3897
                                                        CIP

Published by VGM Career Horizons, a division of NTC Publishing Group
4255 West Touhy Avenue
Lincolnwood (Chicago), Illinois 60646-1975, U.S.A.
© 1994 by Charles C. Prugh. All rights reserved.

To my wife, Eleanor, and our daughters:
Jennifer Sarah, Rebecca Kathryn, and Stephanie Laura

Contents

Waking Up: Coping with Change

1

Early in my years as a career consultant, I discovered one inescapable fact: if you intend to maintain a vibrant, active career throughout your life, you must be aware of what's happening in the business world, throughout your industry or profession, and to and within the company you work for. In addition, you must understand how you feel about what you are doing and be aware of your own changing internal needs, interests, and values in relation to your job or career.

Just what does this mean? It means that the direction the economy and your company is heading may put your job or career in jeopardy. Your position itself may get stuck in a rut, or your internal needs, interests, and values may change so your job or career no longer gives you satisfaction and just isn't going where you want it to.

Becoming aware of each and every one of these factors involves a process I call "waking up." You may think everyone knows something about each of these factors, but the truth is that some people know instinctively that their job or career has veered off course while others don't or simply aren't ready to acknowledge it. I find that many people do not see what's happening to them because of the constant hassle and stress of the business world. It's almost like they've become hypnotized to what's going on and don't realize their job or career is in jeopardy or that they can do better if they only become aware of the problem, and take charge of their work life.

Is this "waking up" process important? You bet it is. It may also turn out to be a life or death matter in some cases. In my work as a career consultant, every day I see the consequences of not being aware of what's happening around or within you. Here are a few examples:

- A middle manager at a Silicone Valley high-tech company lost his job when the company eliminated his department. During the twelve months it took for him to find another position, he lost his wife and his home.

- A food industry middle manager with 15 years of experience wound up taking a $15,000 salary cut when the company merged two departments.

- A retail store manager discovered he was no longer managing the store when the company transferred all of his authority to headquarters. The result was a complete career stagnation.

- A crackerjack salesman discovered his company had stranded him in a boring, dissatisfying sales job in an outlying territory simply because no one else could do well there. They made it quite clear that he would be there another 15 or 20 years.

- A long-time employee of a major company developed ulcers because of the tremendous pressure generated by her present job. Her only choice: quit or put up with it.

- An executive of a major company had two nervous breakdowns directly attributable to her job, yet she refused to quit because the prestige of the position was more important to her than anything else.

The purpose of this chapter is to help you take charge of your life and to become aware of everything that will affect your career. It will also help you update and rewrite your life workscript so as to remain open and ready to consider new challenges in whatever unexpected form they present themselves. Now, let's take a look at the problem and the solutions in some detail.

The Changing Company/Employee Relationship

The last few years, relationships between companies and employees have changed radically. At one time, if an employee was loyal to that company, then that company—in most cases—remained loyal to that employee. In some cases, several generations of family worked in succession for the same company. For the white-collar worker, the dream was that after total loyalty to the company, he or she would receive a big salary and someday a good retirement—a form of lifetime job security.

Today, this atmosphere has been replaced with one in which companies and even whole industries are scrambling to survive. Now we hear of takeovers, restructuring, downsizing, and streamlining. In reality, many companies are furiously trimming their middle management staff. As a result, thousands are suddenly finding themselves jobless. For instance, Verna, 29, lost her job as a marketing manager of a Midwest bakery when the company eliminated her department. Three weeks earlier, she had received the highest possible rating from her supervisor in an annual review. When her boss told her she was losing her job, she laughed. "It's a good joke," she told him, "now what do you really want to see me about?"

Unfortunately, her boss wasn't joking. "It seems, " she told me in our first interview, "that even though my department was making money, they needed to cut back expenses somewhere. My department was their first choice." For the next few weeks, Verna went through a series of emotional stages that resemble an individual's reaction to death or divorce. After the shock comes anger, grief, and, finally, an acceptance of the inevitable. When I saw her in my office, she was still shaken up.

In another example, Toni Thomas, after working her way up from reporter to editor, had been appointed publisher of two advertising-industry publications. She now had an apartment in San Francisco and a weekend condominium at Lake Tahoe. "Our circulation was way up," she told me, "and so was our advertising lineage. We were doing so well that I had just signed up for a long cruise and beefed up my sales staff." Then Toni's boss called her into his office and told her the bad news—this was to be her last day. She was given until the end of the day to fire her staff—just 65 minutes away—and until the end of the week to clean out her own desk.

"It seems," she told me, "that the board of directors were facing a slowdown in advertising and a slowdown in the publishing industry in general. Although my publications were the fastest growing, they also were the last to be added, and would be operating at a slight loss for the next two years. It came down to the fact that if they lopped off my section, they would save a bundle. And that was that."

Today, scenes like these are occurring over and over. Worktrends editor Dan Lacey estimates that in the next 20 years, 70 percent of job layoffs will take place among white-collar workers. Over the same period of time, companies will try to come to grips with the changing business world and begin to streamline their structures.

To anyone whose goal is to have a productive, satisfying career, the challenge is to wake up to what's going on and to take action before it's too late. The question, of course, is how do you wake up to the fact that you may soon be a casualty? The first step is to understand that there is no security today. It all depends on how well a company is doing; if you work for someone else, you are always subject to the whims of the people who employ you. If it's a publicly-held company, the bottom line is what counts, not the years of dedicated service.

Many workers already understand this. A recent study by Brooks International, a management consulting firm, found that fewer than 24 percent of the 11,000 workers surveyed expressed confidence in the long-term future of their jobs. As a result, some employees now make it a habit to keep a resume updated and to interview with other companies every four or five months.

Not all employees will be laid off as companies merge, streamline, and downgrade. However, when this does happen, the entire atmosphere changes. Morale problems arise when management breaks important clauses in an unwritten contract. Employees think that if hard work and loyalty no longer guarantee the payback of security, why should they put the company interest before their own? In addition, for a long time after any change, many of the remaining employees will be on edge, expecting the ax. In some cases, however, there are positive aspects to streamlining: new career paths, less bureaucracy, and greater efficiency. Today, the more progressive companies have begun to recognize the importance and advantage in empowering employees. Some companies, however, centralize their power and try to exercise more control in the changing times.

No matter what kind of organization you now work for, you need to wake up and determine exactly what kind of situation you are in. Now I want to introduce you to two of my clients who have faced such problems.

Nancy, 36, is working for a company that went through a series of shakeups that resulted in layoffs of over 50 percent of the work force. "All of us were positive we were next," she told me. "I'm not sure any of us put in a solid day's work while this was going on." After the third shakeup, Nancy was put in charge of a reorganized department that combined a number of functions that had been performed before by widely separated groups. "This literally gave me a new career," Nancy told me in an interview. "I had to scramble to keep up for a few months, but now I have twice as much authority as I did before, and my salary has doubled."

In our evaluation, we decided that Nancy has a fairly bright future with her company. In addition, she has acquired new skills that she could use to find a job within her field with several other companies and at a level much higher than the one she occupied when the company shakeups occurred.

Another one of my clients, George, 46, had been the branch manager of a major bank for nine years. To get there he had gone through the bank training program and spent years working his way up. Just as he started to look forward to exercising some creative control and to putting some of his own ideas into operation, the bank went through a downsizing and began to change the emphasis of the entire organization.

"For more than a year," he told me, "I've watched the bank centralize all real management at the Los Angeles headquarters, which has gradually reduced the control of the branch managers. At first I was just dissatisfied; gradually, it's become an obsession with me."

What's left of George's job requires him to handle only a few dull, repetitive tasks. "I began to accept the fact," George said, "that branch managers no longer manage the branches. Today I would be embarrassed to tell a local business owner that I could be his personal banker—it wouldn't be true. I took a long hard look at my banking career and concluded that I was only a generalist. I know a little bit about a lot of things, but nothing in depth about anything. Painful for me to admit, but true."

At this point, George was not only dissatisfied with his career but also with his life. He believes that he should have taken stock of his career long ago. "One thing I have realized about the new bank management policy," George said, "is that if an employee doesn't complain and doesn't show ambition to become better, management lets him or her swing in the wind. Now I must do something for myself that I should have been working on a couple of years ago."

A Conflict in Career Goals

Probably a more common problem is when an individual's needs, interests, and values have changed, and he or she is no longer in line with the needs and goals of a particular company.

For instance, Mark, 44, came to me several years ago complaining that his life and career were on dead center. "For five years," Mark told me, "I've been an outside sales representative for the Ogden Mills Company in San Pedro, California. Each day I drive in bumper-to-bumper traffic from my home in Glendale to the plant. That one-way, 70-mile drive is a killer. I arrive exhausted. It's even worse when I get home again at about 8:00 p.m."

Every morning after Mark checks in, he starts calling on his retail customers within a 150-mile radius to sell them as many cartons of canned milk as they will take. Mark admits that often they don't want and can't afford it, but they take it out of loyalty to him. Customers like Mark, however, because he's honest and provides good service. His manager likes him because he's never lost a retail client.

"But my job," he says, "is at a standstill. I feel like I'm running around and around in an endless circle." I asked him about getting a different job in the same company. "Not a chance. If you're good at your job, management doesn't promote you. They want to keep you in place."

Clearly, Mark has awakened to many of his dissatisfactions. He knows he is under considerable strain and he knows he needs to make changes in his life—the sooner, the better. Mark emphasized that he knew the importance of staying awake to his needs, and that if he doesn't, he may find it even harder to escape. He's already beginning to ask himself, "What should I do now?"

Mark is quite capable of making changes in his job, even though he doesn't yet know what changes to make. Awake and aware of his potential, he can now begin to seek a way to hitch up his wagon and get on to the next horizon.

Changing Internal Needs

After a few years of working on the same job at the same company, many of us go to sleep. We arrive at work at the same time every day, go through the same motions, know all the problems, and provide the same solutions every day.

At this point, the zest and enjoyment we felt that first day on the job are gone. Back then, we were eager to get to work, excited to accept new challenges, and happy to be a member of a vital mission. But after a while, one of two things (or a combination of both) happens: We become restless and dissatisfied, or we try to cope with the forces on our job that we can't control.

Diane, 39, had worked for the same company as a secretary for 12 years. For most of this time she was content to just drift along and let the company dictate the direction she was going. Some of the jobs they assigned her were boring, but she never complained. "I will never forget the day I turned 30," she says. "There I was sitting at my desk doing the same thing I had been doing for 12 years when my thoughts flashed ahead 10 years. I saw myself still working for this company, doing the same things, and waiting for the company to decide to promote me to a job I really wanted."

What happened next was even more amazing. Diane's thoughts flashed backward over the past 12 years. Cringing with embarrassment, she admitted for the first time that she had been passive for too long, waiting to be pushed ahead by the company. "Then," she explained, "my thoughts flashed to 'now' and I decided to get some of the things I really wanted. I had always wanted to be an executive secretary—expected that if I worked hard, that's where I would wind up with this company. Now I realized it would never happen. I had the experience, so I had to take charge and push; this probably meant getting another job with a different company."

Diane's skills were such that she could expect to get such a job right now. Her way of waking up, however, was rather simplistic and unique. She changed her relationship to time and to herself. Instead of waiting for the future, she chose the present, and instead of being passive, she decided to become actively responsible for her own future.

I have clients who become stuck in dead-end jobs, and others who have developed skills and knowledge their jobs never let them use. Once they wake up and understand what's happening, many can and do get themselves recharged, sometimes getting their careers going again in their present company. Some, however, must change companies or professions. To realize their full potential, others must change careers from one industry to another or start their own business.

A conclusion that is worth repeating: whether you feel you will wake up in time or too late is not as important as how you interpret it. In my practice, many of my clients have discovered that their interpretation of waking up provided the key to future success. Many of these same clients conclude that waking up is never too late. They are the ones who repeatedly redefine and pursue new goals, which increases their prospects of success. Most of the time, when people realize that they have a greater future than they are currently achieving, they resolve to do something about it.

Unfortunately, not all people feel this way. For instance, some decide that their present salary will prevent them from starting over, or that an employer will feel they are too old to hire. Some people feel waking up is a negative because they haven't kept their skills current. Interpreting work and life experiences negatively will not only dash hopes but will often paralyze efforts to create career opportunities that offer tremendous satisfaction.

For instance, Harry, 52, a design engineer, would simply never take personal responsibility for changing his work style. Harry has been designing miniature equipment for Lockheed for 15 years. He discovered early in his career that he really didn't enjoy engineering. "It was," he said, " too detailed, too conservative, and too structured. In addition, I find engineers a dull bunch." Waking up to your dissatisfactions early is one thing, doing something about them is another. "I got married at an early age," he told me. "Now I must see our three kids through college. I'm 52 years old—it's too late to change. I guess I'll simply grin and bear it until I retire."

Working adults, like Harry, never wake up enough to consciously accept their dissatisfactions. Sometimes they fake their real feelings. They say that someday they will do what they really want to do, but not now. Others refuse to accept the fact that their company may lay them off or their industry may cease to exist, forcing them to make changes.

Such people stifle their vision and their aspirations. Because they are not confident of their ability to succeed, they often become afraid to even think about losing their job or to strike out in another direction. They are the ones that get hit hardest when they lose their job. Sometimes they resign themselves to accepting their lot in life. I hear a lot of excuses. "Life isn't fair. I didn't get the breaks. My boss had it in for me. I got trapped in a dead-end field." They have settled for unchallenging and unrewarding work. In the case of a layoff without preparation, they may go years before they find another job that uses their talents and abilities. These people will never know the exhilaration that comes from experiencing peak performance. That is the price they pay for refusing to take the necessary risks.

Waking Up: The Initial Stages

At this point, waking up means to rouse yourself from performing your responsibilities and the day-to-day activities long enough (1) to become aware of what's happening within the overall economy and the industry; (2) to make sure your company is taking you in the direction you want to go; and (3) to look within yourself to make sure you are growing in ways that meet your current needs, interests, and values. Often you will suddenly realize that you are dissatisfied with the tasks you've been asked to handle for too long.

Now let's start taking stock of your career field, your company, and your internal needs to see where you are right now.

Taking Stock of What's Happening Around You

First, you must determine your job security. One way to do this is to look at the overall health of your industry. Is the industry slowing down, or is it about to slow down in the near future? Today, industries may go through what is called a rolling recession. Real estate is up for a few years, then it is in trouble. Workers on Wall Street do well, then they go through bad times. The same thing happens in other fields.

Next, look at your company. Is it deeply in debt because of a merger, acquisition, or leveraged buyout? Currently, 26 percent of cash flow in many companies goes to debt payments. As the economy goes down, some companies will simply not be able to keep up debt payments and will slip into bankruptcy. There are several warning signs:

1. The company has tried non-layoff alternatives such as hiring freezes and early-retirement programs, and is still in trouble.

2. Your expense checks and/or commissions aren't being paid as quickly as usual.

3. The company is not paying its bills.

4. The company is doing less advertising.

5. Another department is doing much of the work that yours used to do.

6. Your supervisors are getting fired.

7. Management is coping with changing consumer interest in their products or services.

8. A loss of market share occurs because of competitors' actions or foreign competition.

9. You're not getting all the memos you'd expect.

10. Building maintenance services stop watering your plants.

11. Your firm merges with another that duplicates your work.

All of the above are signs that you should wake up and take direct charge of your career. How to do this will be discussed in detail in a later chapter.

If you discover four or five signs that indicate your industry is in trouble, you should consider it carefully and question your bosses and coworkers. Read industry trade journals and newspapers. Many of the major stock brokerage firms have specialists in various industries that can give you informed opinions on what's happening in the industry. You'll find these listed in the New York Yellow Pages. Contact the individual who handles research on your industry to answer your questions or to send you an industry report. In addition, be sure to ask questions among your coworkers—the grapevine may offer a lot of valid information.

After this, rate your current job security on a scale of 0–10. This gives you an informed guess. However, you may be surprised after you've done a little footwork just how accurate your predictions will be.

Taking Stock of Your Work Environment, Your Company, and Yourself   Next, you should set aside time to discover how you feel about your present job, the satisfactions and dissatisfactions you associate with it, and the opportunities your company offers you for personal growth and career advancement. Also, consider how management treats you now and how they may do so in the future. This is the second stage of "waking up."

A good place to start is by writing down your feelings about your present job or career. You can do that by completing the "Self-Inventory of Your Present Work Environment" on the following pages. Record your feelings about items that you can control and for which you are now responsible. Also record your feelings about forces that are out of your control. Nothing is too minor—list everything. Don't try to enter all of your feelings on the self-inventory form. Write your answers in detail on a separate sheet of paper. Include all of the items you would like to change.

After you have finished, write a two-paragraph summary on how you feel about working with your present company. Enter your comments on the "Personal Career Inventory" form on pages 14–15. The summary will help you decide if you are happy, unhappy, or on dead center. It will also help you determine if you can do something to revitalize your career within your present company or if you should consider making some changes.

Self-Inventory of Your Present Work Environment

Work Environment	Improve	Change	No longer care about	Resolve to escape from
Lack of, or not enough recognition from, my present supervisor or manager	_____	_____	_____	_____
Lack of opportunity to acquire status in my present job or career	_____	_____	_____	_____
Lack of a positive environment	_____	_____	_____	_____
Lack of professional knowledge and/or technology required to do my work	_____	_____	_____	_____
Lack of specific projects and self-satisfying goals	_____	_____	_____	_____
Lack of opportunities for professional growth	_____	_____	_____	_____
Lack of management interest in receiving suggestions and criticisms	_____	_____	_____	_____
Lack of management interest in employees' suggestions for improvement of company, products, or services	_____	_____	_____	_____
Lack of evidence that management respects and adopts employees' recommendations and criticisms	_____	_____	_____	_____
Lack of organization	_____	_____	_____	_____
Lack of communication to/from local, not regional, headquarters	_____	_____	_____	_____
Lack of management's interest in developing and maintaining a constructive image in the community	_____	_____	_____	_____
Lack of training programs to develop and motivate employees to a higher level of interest, position, and performance	_____	_____	_____	_____
Other dissatisfying forces and factors about my work environment:				
_____				
_____	_____	_____	_____	_____

Kind and Level of Work

Lack of personal and professional challenges

———— ———— ———— ————

Lack of personal and professional goals that I need to accomplish but cannot accomplish in this company/organization

———— ———— ———— ————

Lack of opportunities to travel

———— ———— ———— ————

Lack of enough time for my personal life

———— ———— ———— ————

Lack of freedom, authority, and responsibility to do my job right

———— ———— ———— ————

Lack of an assigned supervisor or manager to turn to for support when I need it

———— ———— ———— ————

Lack of an adequate salary compared with other employees doing the same kind of work

———— ———— ———— ————

Lack of an adequate compensation package

———— ———— ———— ————

Lack of medical benefits

———— ———— ———— ————

Lack of company training required to do the job

———— ———— ———— ————

Lack of the state-of-the-art equipment and/or systems required to do my job right

———— ———— ———— ————

Lack of an incentive pay arrangement

———— ———— ———— ————

Lack of personal, department, or company objectives

———— ———— ———— ————

Lack of opportunity for flex time

———— ———— ———— ————

Lack of childcare facilities or credits

———— ———— ———— ————

Lack of company policy to reimburse me for completion of work-related credit courses

———— ———— ———— ————

Lack of any good reason to continue to work for my present employer

———— ———— ———— ————

Other dissatisfying forces about the kind and level of work I do:

————————————————————

———————————————————— ———— ———— ———— ————

Work Location

Lack of a convenient work location	_____	_____	_____	_____
Lack of clean workplace air	_____	_____	_____	_____
Lack of reserved, safe, and convenient parking spaces	_____	_____	_____	_____
Lack of proper lighting	_____	_____	_____	_____
Other specific dissatisfying forces	_____	_____	_____	_____

Now for a final "waking-up" survey, you should look within yourself.

Taking Stock of Your Personal and Career Needs, Interests, and Values

As you go along in life, your needs, interests, and values may change. You may acquire new kinds and levels of knowledge, abilities, and skills that you apply or develop in new ways. Sometimes these changes represent personal growth for you in your present job and allow you to add a new dimension to what you are presently doing. At other times, however, you realize that, to fully express your abilities, you need to work for another company, change fields completely, or develop your own business. The inventory below will help you sum up major conclusions about yourself and what is important to you. Answer each question as completely as you can.

Personal Career Inventory

1. I have recently experienced major changes in my attitudes and interests, including personal, social, or spiritual values. This also includes my financial needs or objectives:

   _____

   _____

   _____

   _____

   _____

2. These major changes led me to the following conclusions about what is most important to me in my life and work. (Take some time to think this out thoroughly before answering.) They are:

_____

_____

_____

_____

_____

3. My summary convinces me that I have outgrown, or am no longer challenged by, my present job or career, and that I am ready for a change of responsibilities and/or career direction. (Select one or more of the choices below.)

_____   a. I want to explore additional possibilities with my present employer.

_____   b. I don't want to work with my present employer anymore. I would like to find opportunities with another employer or in another profession.

_____   c. I want to explore a completely different kind of job or career, or look for a different level of work in my present career.

_____   d. I would like to consider developing some form of self-employment.

_____   e. At this point in my life, I would like to consider what it would be like to be a consultant.

Finally, using all of the information you now have about yourself, prepare a personal summary of your feelings about your life and work. Listen to your inner voice—give it plenty of time for full expression. Write down whatever comes to mind: your insights, dissatisfactions, and observations. Your conclusions will become your ongoing "compass," one that will help you stay on course while you search for, find, recognize, negotiate for, or create the right kind and level of work for the rest of your life.

Say "Hello" to the "Real You"

Early in my years as a career consultant, I discovered a second inescapable fact: if you intend to maintain a vibrant, active career throughout your life, you must take stock of what is most important to you now. Taking stock of yourself means to sum up your feelings and convictions about the needs, interests, values, strengths, and accomplishments that are important to you now. Include changes, if any, that you want to make in any of these areas now or in the near future. Having done that, you will have completed the first major step toward jumpstarting your job or career.

***Taking Stock of
Yourself Produces Many
Expected and
Unexpected Benefits***

In my practice, clients who take stock of their needs, interests, values, strengths, and accomplishments enhance their awareness and appreciation of their own worth and achievements. Their conclusions about themselves often becomes the foundation from which they take their next constructive steps. Taking stock of your life and work is especially important when you confront major turning points or have to resolve crises.

Begin by considering examples of the definitions provided by some of my clients below. Of course, you are the only one who can determine your needs, interests, values, strengths, and accomplishments; however, the definitions below may help you define yours.

My Self-Introduction to My "Real Me"

Examples of "Needs"	**Important Needs for Me**	
	Yes	**No**

–Frank, 42, a sales representative for an office supplies retailer, said he needed to escape from a commission-only job because poor sales prevented him from paying his business and personal expenses.

                                   _____   _____

–Lisa, 28, a marketing representative for a Northern California diamond jewelry distributor, needed a position offering more daily contacts with her peers and customers. Being alone and driving long hours each week was beginning to depress her.

                                   _____   _____

–Jane, 48, a nurse working night shifts for two major urban hospitals, needed to find one day-shift position to relieve herself from her present physical overwork and mental stress.

                                   _____   _____

Enter your definitions of needs you'd like met now. Consider ones that will relieve financial, physical, or mental stress or overwork of one kind or another:

_____

_____

Examples of "Interests"	**Important Interests for Me**	
	Yes	**No**

–Bert, 43, an ex-banker, applied for a position as a consultant with a company that provides consulting services to banks. He's interested in this position because he wants to provide solutions for problems he knows the banks have.

                                   _____   _____

–Craig, 26, former advertising account representative on a low, fixed income with no prospects of financial advancement is interested in becoming a real estate sales representative. Here, he can apply his demonstrated sales skills to generate more income and be paid based on his performance, not on management's whims.

Examples of "Interests"

Important Interests for Me

    Yes   **No**

–Laura, 41, former director of a 50-employee medical association, became interested in specializing in the expanding field of preparing and updating compensation and benefits packages for professional health care executives. Her goal: become a consultant and increase her income.

_____   _____

Enter your definitions of interests you'd like to research, develop, and apply. Consider ones that will give you an outlet for your knowledge, experience, special abilities, or skills, even for making good use of the many personal contacts you have or can develop:

_____

_____

Examples of "Values"

Important Values for Me

    Yes   **No**

–Ruth, 38, a public relations consultant, resolved to promote causes she believed in, ones that would benefit society, not merely promote businesses or products. She sought a position as a public relations officer for a nonprofit organization that provides environmental education materials for the public.

_____   _____

–Stanley, 43, a CPA and former controller of a multinational corporation, resolved to find employment for a growth-committed American-owned manufacturing company pursuing ways to expand their sales into international markets. Placing a high value on "people-oriented" managements that promote teamwork among employees, he wanted to play a major role in the company's growth.

_____   _____

–Judy, 41, a former judge in juvenile court, resigned from her position to accept a lower paying, lower prestige role in state government. She valued state-funded programs for AIDS patients and their families and believed her experience could help state government design and pass better bills for this purpose.

_____   _____

Enter your definitions of personal, social, and/or spiritual values you'd like to act from or pursue. Consider ones that will introduce needed and better changes in society in one way or another:

_____

_____

The purpose of this chapter is to help you begin to get in touch with what is really important to you now, to say "hello" to the "real you." When you are grounded in what is important to you now, you are much better prepared to evaluate the pros and cons of your present position; you are better equipped to define and pursue new objectives and to recognize worthwhile ones when they appear; and you are more confident as you explore new challenges and opportunities in whatever unexpected form they appear. Acting from your summary of the "real you," you more easily move ahead on your pathway to finding, creating, or regaining the zest and enjoyment you want and expect from your job or career.

Staying Vital Your First Step Is to Become Aware that You Are Not at Home with Yourself

The first step toward saying "hello" to the "real you" is to step back from the demands and expectations of your present or most recent job or career and to ask yourself four questions:

Questions

1. What major changes do I see occurring in my present or most recent job or career that threaten to reduce the zest and enjoyment I receive—or received—from it?

2. What new or major changes in my own personal needs, interests, values, strengths, or accomplishments are occurring, or have recently occurred, in my own life now? Ones that seriously detract from my continuing interest in remaining or advancing in my present or most recent job or career, or in my present industry or organization?

3. What optional directions, or decisions, can I imagine myself pursuing, or making, that would help me regain or create new zest and enjoyment from my job or career?

4. Will I accept personal responsibility for persevering in my efforts to translate my current self-definition into another kind and/or level of job or career direction?

My Answers

_____

_____

_____

_____

Your answers to these four questions will enable you to become more conscious of what really is important to you about your life and work right now. Your answers will remind you of the extent of continuing effort that you will need if you are to become successful in regaining or creating zest and enjoyment from your work. Whether you answer these questions quickly and easily, or slowly and through a period of painful personal readjustment, you are taking your second major step toward saying "hello" to the "real you."

There are two very good reasons for answering questions one through four, now and at major turning points during your lifetime:

1. After we have worked at the same job for many years, or after we have long been in the same profession, we fall into the belief that the structure of our job or profession tends to define our identity. We conclude that we *are* whatever we presently *do.* Answering questions about our identity helps us develop useful objectivity about what we are *independently* of what we do. The more we are aware of our needs, interests, values, strengths, and accomplishments, the more *independence* we acquire during times of major changes.

Other people seem to accept us on the basis of what they believe we do. We may receive recognition, prestige, self-esteem, and economic security from our derived identity. And, we are tempted to combine our job title and personal identity if we work for a "name" individual or organization, or if we have what might be regarded as a "prestigious" or "glamorous" position or profession.

2. We change. We change constantly in major and minor ways. We modify and/or abandon long-cherished needs, interests, values, strengths, and accomplishments in one way or another to varying degrees.

Our derived identity, however, is a two-edged sword. On one side, as long as we like it and derive acceptable rewards from it, we remain content. On the other side, if we begin to question the value of that derived identity, and begin to give it up and yearn for "something better," we find ourselves moving into a period of great personal uncertainty about who we really are independently of that job or career. We also find ourselves deciding what is most important to us, perceiving what we could possibly do next, and discovering alternative jobs or careers that will enable us to become gainfully employed with a minimum of adjustment.

For these two reasons, you will quickly discover the value of beginning to conduct your own self-evaluation and self-summary. Soon you will discover that your efforts produce exciting results; you will "give yourself permission" to speak your own mind, perhaps for the first time; you will experience insights into your own reasons and needs for changes or for updating personal needs, interests, values, strengths, and accomplishments; and soon you will begin to define and explore new challenges and opportunities, sometimes even create your own.

In my experience, those who report success in their efforts at self-clarification act more decisively and with greater personal conviction. They believe more things are possible for them than they first thought. They believe they can accomplish more through their own efforts than they had deemed admissable. They believe they are more likely to achieve goals if they have goals to pursue. They believe they are more likely to influence events to their advantage than they first thought possible.

All these new attitudes and strengthened beliefs are among the benefits that accrue from getting in touch with the "real you." If you feel that you and your job or career are so closely interwoven that you find it hard to separate the "real you" from your job, career, or organization, if you feel uncomfortable separating the "real you" from the enticing status, benefits, or security that you find or have found in your present or most recent job or career, if you have made major changes in your needs, interests, values, strengths, or accomplishments that chart you in a new and uncertain direction away from your present or most recent job or career, this chapter will help you take charge of your life and work and begin to make necessary changes.

You might wonder if everyone, at one time or another, experiences boredom, lack of satisfaction, or lack of personal, social, financial, and spiritual rewards, from his or her work. Certainly, but my clients are people who are trying to resolve or surmount such conditions; they are trying to move up, over, or out of their job or career; and they are determined to find or create work that meets their standards. They succeed in their endeavor because they persevere in their pursuit until they find or create it.

Saying "Hello" to the "Real You" in Different Ways

Daily, I meet many people with different kinds of jobs and careers, locally and nationwide. Many admit their present or most recent job or career lacks features and/or benefits that they would like to have. They readily discuss the features and benefits they would like more of as well as the forces and/or factors they would like less of.

We begin the process of making changes—jumpstarting their job or career to one degree or another—by clarifying their degree of satisfaction, or of dissatisfaction, with each of the six factors below. We focus on the factor(s) they are trying to change, and, if possible, change them or develop a plan for changing them, now or at the right time.

Factors	Favorable	Unfavorable
1. The kind of work they perform or have performed	_____	_____
2. The work environment. Includes		
–size of the organization	_____	_____
–management style	_____	_____
–purpose	_____	_____
–annual sales volume	_____	_____
–reputation	_____	_____
–headquarters location	_____	_____
–dress code	_____	_____
–career advancement prospects	_____	_____
–changes rumored or in process	_____	_____
–their interest or lack of interest	_____	_____
3. Working among adults in the organization who recognize and respect their talents and goals and vice versa	_____	_____
4. For the right personal, social, and spiritual rewards	_____	_____
5. The physical location of the worksite: includes the neighborhood, parking spaces, lighting, and safety	_____	_____
6. The round-trip daily commute: includes distance, time required, driving conditions, and method of transportation	_____	_____

In my experience, people who succeed in saying "hello" to the "real you" are the ones who have succeeded in re-aligning one, some, or all of factors one through six. The new alignment of factors gives them a greater sense of control over factors that are a part of their job or career. They've arranged to have more of their needs met; they've identified major interests and are better positioned to develop and apply them; and they've located positions or challenges they value. Combined, they feel they are in touch with themselves and their skills and act from them to achieve valued goals.

You too may need to say "hello" to the "real you." If so, begin by checking the factors that are favorable or unfavorable. After you have done that, you will have completed the third step in recognizing the forces and factors you want to change.

Changing the Kind of Work Performed

Some people say "hello" to their "real you" by revising only factor no. 1: the kind of work they are doing.

Audrey, 26, former supervisor of four employees in a retail electronics equipment store, is a good example of someone who wasn't in touch with what was really important to her. When she began summing up and surmounting some of her uncertainties she gradually became aware of subjects she liked to work on and skills she liked to apply. Her excitement grew as she realized she could develop her career upward if she pursued both an educational and an employment objective.

"In three years, I worked myself up from clerk to supervisor in a high-volume, constantly expanding retail store," she told me. "Sometimes my manager assigned me to do other jobs when employees were absent. Now I have experience as a receptionist, inventory control clerk, accounts payable clerk, supervisor, and bookkeeper. Recently my boss demoted me to sales clerk because business is slow. I had worked so hard to be promoted to supervisor that I hadn't taken time or energy to think much about what I really want to do. Now I'm bored."

Clearly, Audrey took a good look at her job and recognized that she had to find and pursue a specific kind of work that interested her. This was necessary in order for her to regain the zest and excitement she felt while working to become a supervisor and, in fact, while she was a supervisor. She has no interest in other factors connected with her job.

Highly motivated people like Audrey often most quickly identify the specific kind of work they want to do if I work with them to list all of the jobs they have performed, including present and past employers; discuss each job both positively and negatively; and compare the satisfactions they received from each job. From such a focused approach to comparison and evaluation, it's often easy to identify one or more jobs that were better than the others. Audrey quickly came to her own conclusion: "Now that I've set aside the time to think about all the jobs I've done, I like bookkeeping best of all. I have discovered that recording and studying numbers is exciting; they tell you where the company has been and show you where it may be going. I found myself looking ahead and wondering what we should be doing to expand the business. Another thing, I like to work independently, not as a supervisor with a lot of people around me. Posting, entering data in the computer, and preparing reports was like studying the business."

Audrey got in touch with her "real you"—working alone with figures, analyzing information, writing reports, and learning more about accounting—after she had taken the time to think about her work. Audrey was now grounded in conclusions about herself from which she could plan her career. She decided to enroll in community college courses in bookkeeping, accounting, and computer operations. Her educational objective is to complete a four-year degree in business management. "Who knows?" she exclaimed the last time I saw her. "I might even decide to become a C.P.A.!"

Because of these and many other benefits that accrue to people like Audrey, I always encourage new clients to begin their process of making personal changes by first summing up what is really important to them now in their life and work. From self-examination, they become clearer about what is important to them and what they want to change. A good way to begin to set aside a time for self-reflection is to reserve what German philosopher Fredrich Nietsche called a "niche of silence." I urge my clients to create their own "niche of silence" to allow themselves time and opportunity to say "hello" to their "real you." Audrey's "niche of silence" encouraged the thoughtful self-appraisal that produced her own insights into what she liked to do best and why.

You too may need to sum up the responsibilities you've had and the skills you've used during one or several periods of employment. If so, begin by listing your present or most recent job or career, emphasizing the last 5–10 years. Include responsibilities and skills used in volunteer work or hobbies. Write down the responsibilities and skills you've liked most of all by copying the following data sheet and entering your observations, explaining why you liked them. Create your own "niche of silence": ask yourself if you'd like to exercise the same responsibilities and skills but in a different way. Your answers will help you become conscious about your interests, abilities, skills, and values.

DATA SHEET

Dates	Co./Org. (Paid Employment)	Volunteer/Hobby or Other Activities	What Did I Do?	What Interests/ Abilities/Values Did I Apply In Each Situation?	Results (Good and Bad)	Major Tasks/Features/ Achievements I Enjoyed *Most of All*	What Interests/ Abilities/Values Are Important to Me *Now*?

Combined, they become the cornerstone for your plan to jumpstart your job or career; they will motivate you to make major changes at the right time.

Changing the Work Environment

Some people say "hello" to their "real you" by revising only factor no. 2: the environment they work in.

Barbara, 31, former director of product development for a Fortune 500 corporation, wasn't in touch with what was really important to her—her "real you"—but made impressive progress while listening to both her inner voice and her boss's evaluation of her performance. "While he was telling me how great I was, I was mentally reverse-and-fast-forwarding my career path from college to now," she said. "Oh, I heard my boss, but my mind was looking for new conclusions, a better place to land, a different 'center' for my life."

Barbara was opening the door to new adventures. She was beginning to ask herself what kind of person she wanted to be. She also began to shed the role of "corporate career woman" and to experience her own "real you." Her notes in her career journal further enabled her to clarify what she wanted to be and do. Her summary enabled her to jumpstart her career with new confidence and a sense of purpose. "I summed up my feelings about being a 31-year-old single woman, a high achiever, climbing a corporate ladder that may not exist in a large, male-dominated corporation. The more I wrote about my feelings, the less I liked what I felt." She continued: "A corporation, in my experience, is the ultimate cookie cutter: the employee is the dough. A corporation is faceless; it's really a bunch of self-seeking individuals speaking "corporationese." This is when your boss says 'we believe teamwork is important' (he makes all the decisions) or when your boss says 'creativity is what we look for' (it's okay to come up with ideas now and again, but be sure I like them). As for management's claim that the corporation is socially conscious because it contributes $1,000,000 to a social program, that's nonsense. It means they have donated less than .1% per unit sold. Big deal—not much of a social consciousness as far as I'm concerned."

Barbara, like Audrey, had said "hello" to her "real you," and she had done it in her own unique way: being willing to pay attention to her mind, sum up a lot of feelings, and then express them in writing. Her "niche of silence" had occurred at a most unusual moment: during, of all places, a conversation with her boss!

Acting on her conclusions, Barbara charted a new course and achieved her objectives. "Looking back," she said, "my bosses have always been egotists, quantitative thinkers, politically sophisticated, empire builders in a male-dominated corporate world. As a single, 31-year-old woman, I've had to justify myself and my work, especially when working among males about my age. I've had to be competitive, quantitative, and political; that's the role you play to compete in a faceless corporate environment. So, while my boss was praising me, I was beginning to bail myself out of the corporate world."

As a result of her self-clarification, Barbara had updated her resume, tailored a plan to research medium-sized corporations, and got herself a position as manager of product development. "Teamwork is the primary principle in my present company (200–300 employees, annual sales $50,000,000, headquartered locally). We define teamwork goals and we expect big egos to set examples of ways to accomplish corporate tasks, not build their own empires or show how important they think they are. I've made the right changes. I feel at home with myself for a change. And I feel great!"

You too may want to get in touch with your "real you" by reacting, like Barbara, to Factor 2: the unfavorable work environment. If so, begin your self-clarification by expressing your conclusions about what you want to change. Next, begin to research work environments that are right for you. Like Barbara, knowing what you are trying to change—your work environment—makes it much easier for you to plan and carry out important changes.

Marketing Yourself

Some people say "hello" to their "real you" by using their imagination to present themselves as a "product," and then contact employers likely to hire such a product.

Jill, 35, a former manager of customer sales and service for a major leasing company, got in touch with her "real you"—her *work experience* was most important to her—by organizing and presenting her work experience to market herself as an efficient performer. Having completed her list, she wrote a one-page letter to key managers in the leasing equipment industry. She marketed herself as a "high quality" product.

Jill's letter effectively applied the guidelines recommended by the advocates of "careerism" as the best way to find or create a satisfactory kind of job or career. Such advocates emphasize the importance of standing back, seeing yourself as an 'object,' and presenting yourself as a candidate who can recognize problems, provide solutions, and produce benefits for yourself and your employers. While "careerism" is one effective way to find or create a "right" position, and possibly the most widely used format among jobseekers and career changers today, it is not the only way for many adults. Other ways appear in the stories and examples throughout this book.

Jill's letter appears below:

Dear Sir:

I am writing to introduce myself to you: I have been directly in charge of customer sales and service for a major equipment company leasing to customers locally and nationwide. I have been promoted twice and consistently received both annual and merit increases during my 16½ years of experience.

I am writing to ask if you plan to hire one or more experienced customer sales and/or service representatives now or in the near future. If you do, you will be interested in my experience:

- customer service
- promoting and selling equipment maintenance contracts for electronic and electrical equipment, including supplies
- handling and renewing leasing agreements
- providing product support on-site and over the telephone
- training employees over the telephone
- resolving billing issues
- explaining terms of company contract

Now I am seeking a position where I can apply my experience and contribute to the growth of another major organization. My research among leading leasing companies convinces me that you may now or in the near future need employees in this area.

I will welcome an opportunity to meet with you to discuss our mutual objectives. I will call you next week in the hope of arranging a meeting with you. You may of course call me at any time at (555) 555-5555. Thank you in advance for your interest and response to my inquiry.

Very truly yours,

Jill H.

Clearly Jill is in touch with not only her "real you" but also with prospective employers. She has marketed herself as a goal-directed, results-oriented problem solver.

Jill learned a lot from presenting herself as a marketable product. She learned to emphasize functions, responsibilities, and skills she used for her past employers. The functions she presented were important to any position she would accept in the equipment leasing industry. She also learned to introduce her assets in ways that would show not only her interests in her career but in how her objectives would meet a prospective employer's present or future needs. "My letter helped me target my job search," she said. "As a result, I found my new position in much less time. I had written letters only to 10 corporations that would be interested in me. One of them had a part-time position open, and they offered it to me. I accepted it with the assurance that it would be expanded into a full-time position within six months."

You too may want to step back and sum up your work experience and present yourself as an efficient and effective performer in a short letter of inquiry. If so, begin by preparing a summary of the high-priority functions you have performed. Emphasize ones you want to perform now. Then, using Jill's letter as a guideline, write and address your letters to key managers most likely to be interested in your experience. If you succeed in marketing yourself by attracting the reader's attention, you are likely to find an exciting and challenging position in a short amount of time.

Exploring New Careers

Some people say "hello" to their "real you" by exploring jobs or careers that will give them new outlets for their interests and values.

Some people, taken aback by rejections, unreturned telephone calls, or lack of responses from prospective employers, become restless and begin to apply for positions for which they have little or no required experience. Such positions are often in another industry or special area of the economy. Even so, people explore such openings because they seem exciting, adventurous, even likely to produce great riches with minimal effort. Some positions appear to offer a security that does not exist in peoples' present jobs or careers.

Those who begin to apply for different or unusual positions are also seeking ways to get in touch with their "real you," but they are doing it in a new way. They are beginning to ask themselves questions asked often at critical or major turning points in a job or career pathway:

1. Why not me?

2. Will I be able to learn what I don't know about this position or opportunity?

3. Will my previous experiences help me get started, and could I get up to speed quickly?

4. Can I do or learn to do this job since I have done jobs like it before?

5. Will this job or opportunity offer me the security, independence, and control that my present employer cannot offer me?

You may also be considering openings or opportunities that you want to pursue. Perhaps you perceive fewer opportunities for security, stability, or advancement in your own profession or industry because the restructuring and downsizing of the American work force and economy imply fewer opportunities in the years ahead. If so, begin to ask yourself the above questions as you research and explore opportunities that seem interesting to you. You may discover a job or career that provides an outlet for your enthusiasm, talents, energies, and skills.

Mary Lou, 38, a former eighth-grade teacher, considered different, unusual, even adventurous opportunities that enabled her to work outdoors with motivated adults. Uncertain about what knowledge, skills and experience she could offer employers in other fields, she often repeated questions 1 through 5 to herself as she explored alternative options and opportunities. She literally found her "ideal" job in her own backyard.

"My long-term hobby and avocation has been to work in my own garden," she told me. "My neighbors admired my garden and often came over to see what I was doing. One neighbor, knowing I was unemployed and looking around, asked me to take care of his yard on an hourly basis. Soon other neighbors joined in and I found myself busy taking care of lots of gardens near my home."

Mary Lou was in touch with work that was important to her—her "real you"—and began to wonder how she could do the gardening work satisfactorily and derive an acceptable income from it.

"I soon discovered that there was a lot I didn't know about gardening, and I knew nothing about landscaping. I investigated community college programs and discovered that I could earn a landscaping certificate in one year. I studied and worked hard for one year. By the end of the year, I knew I still loved the work but had to admit that I couldn't handle all of the physical work involved in hauling heavy supplies and equipment into and out of my truck. I knew I could handle low maintenance and drought-resistant plants and shrubbery. So I again asked myself questions 1 through 5 and concluded that I could qualify for employment as a road maintenance gardener for the city government where I live. I easily passed their civil service examination and accepted my present position."

If you are considering opportunities that you might not otherwise select or consider, begin by asking yourself the questions below:

1. What do people in these interesting occupations or professions actually do?

2. What do I need to know to enter one of these occupations or careers?

3. What do I need to know or learn about an occupation or career that interests me now?

4. What would I do with this information? Apply for a position? Complete a training program?

5. Am I willing to work the way people in this occupation or career work?

6. What would be the starting salary for a person with my qualifications?

7. What would it cost me to prepare myself for employment in this occupation or career?

8. What benefits would I receive that are not available at my present occupation or career?

Readjusting Your Relationship   Some people say "hello" to their "real you" by readjusting their relationship with their present job or career.

Harry, 42, a self-employed plumber for many years, realized he could no longer tolerate the hard physical work of his trade. Forced to readjust his relationship with his work, he asked questions 1 through 5 while he investigated positions for a building inspector, an appraiser, and even a marketing representative for a plumbing supply manufacturer. "I soon learned that I would have to pass a county examination to become a certified building inspector. After completing the course, I easily passed the examination. Now I can apply my knowledge and experience without all of the hard work."

If you feel compelled to readjust yourself to your present occupation or career, begin by asking questions 1 through 5 about occupations or careers that are related to your present field. You may discover prospective employers open to your needs and goals.

Taking Stock of Your Life and Work Requires Special Effort

Taking stock of your life and work at this time requires you to be completely honest with yourself. You will evaluate your feelings and beliefs about your present work or profession, including your career decisions to date. You will summarize your feelings about the kind of work you perform, the environment in which you work, and the types of people you work with. You will determine if you and your coworkers have a mutual respect for each other's talents and abilities. Finally, you will discover what personal, social, and spiritual satisfaction you receive from your work at this time of your life. Your evaluations of these and other factors will form conclusions from which you can begin to act in your own best interests and at the right time.

Neglecting to Take Stock of Your Life and Work Is Risky

If you do not set aside a "niche of silence" to give yourself an honest self-definition, you risk settling for whatever work comes your way or whatever work people give you. You also risk becoming bogged down in the same job for weeks, months, even years, each day a monotonous replay of the previous day. You may never know the personal satisfaction and excitement that comes from having taken stock of yourself and having acted in new ways to achieve new and important objectives. You risk never experiencing the renewal and surge of self-confidence and self-esteem that stems from your inner conviction that you are acting from current knowledge of your needs, interest, values, strengths, and accomplishments.

Making Personal Changes: Better Late Than Never

In my practice, some clients seek assistance in revising a low self-image that stems from major disappointments or mistakes in their life. Often, such clients are not acting from an awareness or appreciation of their present personal strengths and goals. Instead, they are living in the past; sometimes they express negative feelings, guilt, dejection, and cynicism about their interpretation of the past. Overcoming this may require them to change their self-image in painful, self-adjusting ways at a late stage in their life. To do this, they often need to learn new habits of self-acceptance so that they can relate more positively to strangers and to their coworkers.

These clients will succeed only if they accept total responsibility for making personal internal changes, only if they can be totally honest with themselves, and only if they persevere in applying their new conclusions about themselves in the ways that I propose. Often, such clients succeed in saying "hello" to their "real you" after days, weeks, even months, of personal trauma. Late they are in making personal readjustments, but late is better than never.

Frank, 51, recently released on parole from San Quentin, shows the pain, progress, and pathway that some of my clients experience as they move through the process of self-rejection to self-acceptance in finding or creating a job or career.

"At night I sleep peacefully now," he wrote in his most recent letter to me. "I spent eight years in San Quentin, serving time for voluntary manslaughter. All those years I was berating myself for having gotten so angry in a bar where I had had too many drinks, got in a fight with a stranger, and hit him over the head with an empty bottle. He fell down and died. Since that night, I've talked myself into believing that no one would ever hire me again."

Formerly a stockbroker, Frank admitted that his life since that night had been a living hell. Sometimes the memory of negative, self-destructive feelings about himself jolts him awake. After his release from prison, he began to seek work but found himself presenting his negative self-image to interviewers and never attracting a job offer. Soon he despaired of ever finding employment. "My wife divorced me while I was in prison, and my kids stopped coming to see me. I concluded that I was just a drunk who had killed a stranger because I couldn't control my anger. When interviewers asked me what I did to get into prison, I told them that I'd hit a stranger over the head with an empty bottle and he fell down and died."

Frank began to recognize that he needed help, and he

accepted responsibility for getting it as he proceeded on his search for employment. He admitted that he did not get second interviews because of the way he described himself. He started to change. He spoke honestly from his real feelings as he described his qualifications and experiences. "When I was being interviewed," he continued in his letter, "the interviewer would ask me a lot of questions about when I was a stockbroker. I answered them clearly and easily. But when the interviewer would ask me why I had been imprisoned, I became trapped by my negative feelings about myself. I would blurt out my version of the truth."

Frank's emerging self-acceptance and interest in the present became stronger as he talked more and more about his job inside the prison. He talked about how he had prepared and adjusted annual budgets, supervised and trained the entire food service operation, and even attracted the personal attention of the warden. Now he was seeking a position as manager of a commercial food service department for a major company, and he had good experience and references. "Gradually I began to give myself credit for the new career I had learned in San Quentin. I spoke of my skills and accomplishments. I admitted past mistakes in my life, ones that I would always regret but couldn't change. I participated in many interviews with employers, even began to get second interviews. Recently I was hired to be the manager of a commercial cafeteria for a Fortune 500 corporation. The interviewer said he liked me for my honesty and for the way I tried to turn my life around while in San Quentin."

Frank, like others who are late in getting in touch with their "real you," succeeded in surmounting his self-image by emphasizing who he was and what he was in the present. He let the past be the past—he could not change it or erase it. Learning to speak highly of himself was a slow and painful process. He learned to revise and strengthen his self-image late, but late is better than never.

Begin to revitalize your present self-image by focusing on your good, constructive intentions in the present, giving yourself credit for pursuing present goals, not dwelling on past failures. Speak knowledgeably and sincerely about goals you want to accomplish and practice acknowledging others who contribute to your efforts along the way. Stop mulling over past events, relationships, or accidents that cannot be changed. Let the past go and don't look back. Be future-oriented; define goals to accomplish and invest your energies in achieving them. Acting on your own behalf, you will succeed in jumpstarting your career. Even though late, late is better than never.

Some People May Never Say "Hello" to Their "Real You"

Some people may never allow themselves to accept personal responsibility for acting on the basis of their honest admissions about themselves. Some cannot accept personal responsibility even when their mental or physical health is at stake. Instead, they remain employed in their present position even if it causes considerable stress.

Bonnie, 46, a bookkeeper for IBM for many years, could never free herself from her dependency on the advantages of her present position. "I will never resign from my position as a bookkeeper for IBM," she said, "even though my job has given me an ulcer. My doctor recommends that I find employment elsewhere, but I won't resign. Working for IBM gives me status, and I like to tell my friends I work for IBM because I know they're impressed."

Bonnie may never get in touch with her "real you" in any way deeper or more mature than her present need for "status" that she receives from working for a "name" company. Sadly, such people seem to remain in their present positions. They appear incapable of aspiring to a higher level of personal maturity and often remain in a job or career that causes them considerable stress and poor physical health.

Summary

Begin to say "hello" to your "real you" by reviewing the varied ways we've discussed in this chapter. Answer the questions that appear in "Self-Introduction to my Real Me" to help you clarify your present needs, interests, and values. Write your own answers to the four questions. Complete your summary of factors that are favorable and unfavorable for you in your job or career. Sum up the responsibilities and skills you most like to perform on the Data Sheet. Combined, your entries and answers on all of the forms will enable you to nurture a lasting friendship by saying "hello" to the "real you."

Making Changes at Exactly the Right Time

In this chapter, we're going to look at why and when you need to know to make major changes so you can act in your own best interests and at the right time.

Why? Because when you make major changes, you need to get the most benefits and greatest rewards from them. Being certain of why and when you make changes increases your prospects of benefiting from them.

Many adults decide to make major changes in their life and work in response to sudden or gradual changes in personal needs, interests, values, or rewards they want to receive; changes introduced by forces and factors over which they have little or no influence or control; or a combination of both.

The "Right Time" May Happen Suddenly

Gloria, 38, is a person who *suddenly* changed. For 10 years, she worked hard to be recognized as the most innovative curriculum planner employed by the state of Nevada. "I introduced many new programs, changed existing ones, and attended many association meetings and conventions," she said. "Not for one moment had I ever thought of resigning my position to seek better-paying employment. I changed my mind when my new husband and I bought a house that needed a lot of work. One day, I realized that I would have to bring in more money and leave the education profession. I decided that, if I were going to work primarily to generate more income, I would try to obtain a position with a company that I admire: IBM."

Gloria's story illustrates the point of this chapter: we change, forces and factors around us change; sometimes we respond to personal internal changes, external changes, or a combination of both. One thing is certain: when you make major changes, you must be sure of the changes you want to make and when you should make them. Acting from personal certainty, you are much more likely to derive the most benefits.

In my practice, I help people recognize major changes by having them prioritize changes that are necessary to make major changes. I design an employment search program that will help them change or advance their present position, seek employment with another organization, or pursue an alternative career direction. I then work with them to apply the program in their own best interests at the right time. This is what we will learn to do in this book.

Gloria's employment search program was designed to help her (1) research and learn about IBM so she would appear knowledgeable and prepared for her interview with IBM; (2) obtain an interview with a key IBM representative, and (3) attract an offer from IBM. To start her program, Gloria first completed the two forms shown on the following pages. This information was used to plan and carry out a strategy that produced not only an interview but also an ideal employment offer.

To complete basic research about a particular company that will prepare you for an employment interview, use either one or both of the forms titled Industry or Profession Evaluation Checklist and the Company Evaluation Checklist. Both will improve your professional self-presentation and your impact on the prospective employer.

Deciding why and when to make major changes is different for everyone. Like Gloria, some may decide quickly; others take days, weeks, even months. Some recognize why they want to change, but decide that now is the not the right time. For these people, now may be the time to *prepare* themselves to make major changes. A few give up, and sadly, conclude that they cannot ever make major changes.

Industry or Profession Evaluation Checklist

Questions worth asking yourself and anyone employed in an industry or profession that you are attempting to investigate, enter, evaluate, or advance in.

Does the industry or profession	Yes	No	Don't Know
have a strong history of growth?	_____	_____	_____
presently show continuing growth?	_____	_____	_____
have a reputation for innovation and technological progress?	_____	_____	_____
have a diversified market (i.e., it does not depend on government or one industry for a high percentage of business volume)?	_____	_____	_____
have a market that offers high potential for growth?	_____	_____	_____
show that it has increased the number of people employed in it during the past five years?	_____	_____	_____
offer women opportunities to fill management positions?	_____	_____	_____
show women now hold top management positions?	_____	_____	_____
offer women salaries that are comparable with their peers in other companies in that industry and/or in other industries?	_____	_____	_____

Company Evaluation Checklist   Date: _____

Company name _____

Address _____

City _____ State _____ Zip _____

Telephone: (   ) _____ FAX _____

Key contact person _____ Title _____

Headquarters location _____

Branch offices (your area) _____

Number of employees _____

Annual reported sales
—national   _____

—international   _____

Management style
—bureaucratic
   _____

—project oriented
   _____

—power downward
   _____

—entrepreneurial
   _____

—market driven
   _____

Percentage of money and
interest invested in R&D
   _____

Product line
—products
   _____

—reputation among users
   _____

—technical
   _____

—nontechnical
   _____

—competitive pricing
   _____

—chosen market area
   _____

—percent of control in chosen market area
   _____

Company goals and evidence they can cite that
shows they are achieving some of them
   _____

Company reputation in its industry
   _____

   _____

   _____

   _____

Department size
   _____

New projects
   _____

Career development policies, practices,
and reputation
   _____

Compensation package
   _____

   _____

The "Right time" May Happen Gradually

Some people change gradually. Duane, 48, a former manager of a large retail store in California, made a major change only after he had become clear about what he was trying to change.

"I've been changing slowly for the past three years, but I'm not sure I know what to do," he said. "I know I can easily get another job, but I don't try to get it."

Duane said he was trying to make his life better, but he wasn't sure what 'better' meant. As a result, he was in a state of mental paralysis. This caused him to get involved in a lot of unfocused and unsatisfying activities. He needed time and the opportunity to express his feelings so he could sum up the most important ones. He needed an employment search program that was quite different from the one that Gloria used.

Duane's program was designed to encourage him to listen to himself and then sum up the major changes he wants to make. "At my age," he said, "I'm trying to get control over my life. I'm entering a new stage. After having recently been laid off and divorced, I'm looking for stability. I no longer want to move from one job or community to another."

People like Duane often search both inward and outward, and review their past life and work experience for core beliefs that were important then and are important now. From such beliefs, they more easily select the major changes to make now.

Since Duane did not want to change his job or industry, he considered changing his geographical environment. "I hate my living environment," he said. "It's a sprawling, suburban, smoggy, bumper-to-bumper traffic town. I only moved here to be with my wife who wanted to live near her parents. I grew up in a tiny town on the slopes of Mt. Rainier where I knew everybody. Now I'm divorced—I can move anywhere."

Those who listen to their feelings get in touch with their interests, values, ideals, and how they feel about their geographical environment. As a result, they often act on these feelings. After Duane reflected on where he'd grown up, he knew what he wanted to do next. "Most of all," he said, "I want to return to a small town in the Pacific Northwest where there are lots of green trees year round." So, he moved there. Soon he got a job as a retail store manager on tree-covered Brekenridge Island on Puget Sound.

Sometimes, people like Duane get off course with their careers. After personal reflection, they reset their compass and chart a new course. After making progress, they see that they have made the right choices; they speak with greater confidence; and they "come home" to their deeper core values, the ones that now give them the stability they were seeking.

If you want to make major changes in your work or geographical environment, begin by completing The Environment form on the next page. You may discover core values and major changes you want to make now or at a time that is right for you.

The Environment

I Want to Make Major Changes in	Yes	No
—geographical location (where I live)	_____	_____
—geographical location (where I work)	_____	_____
—round-trip daily commute to/from home	_____	_____

Size of the area in which I live

	Yes	No
—large urban city	_____	_____
—medium-sized urban area	_____	_____
—small town	_____	_____
—tiny village	_____	_____

Structure

	Yes	No
—established	_____	_____
—expanding	_____	_____
—suburban	_____	_____
—agricultural	_____	_____

Special Characteristics

	Yes	No
—near the seashore	_____	_____
—near the desert	_____	_____
—in a foreign country	_____	_____
—near recreational facilities	_____	_____
—an island	_____	_____
—away from parents, relatives, and friends	_____	_____
—near my parents, relatives, and friends	_____	_____
—a retirement community	_____	_____

—other: _____

_____

Other Major Changes I Would Like to Make in My Environment:

_____

_____

_____

Preparing to Make Major Changes

We've discussed how some people suddenly make career changes and how others make them gradually. Let's look at those who anticipate and prepare for major changes.

Barbara, 44, and her husband Pat, 48, first prepared themselves to become self-employed as a husband-and-wife team; they wanted to operate their own electronic repair business.

"I work for a company that repairs electronic equipment," Pat said. "My boss doesn't care whether we do good work for our customers. My customers have told me they'd hire me to service their equipment if I was self-employed, so I'm looking into it."

Barbara handles the posting and accounts payable for a hardware store, but is not an accountant. "My husband and I want to quit our jobs," she said. "I don't know that much about bookkeeping, but I know I can learn more."

Clients like Barbara and Pat often underestimate the scope and complexity involved in becoming self-employed. They know little about the importance of time management, sales and marketing skills, computer-supported controls, and customer service terms, among other things. As part of their individual program, they first completed the following questionnaire, "Self-Employment: Is It for You Now? Or in the Future?" Their answers helped them identify their strengths and weaknesses, areas for self-improvement, as well as why and when to make the major changes needed to become self-employed.

Self-Employment: Is It for You Now? Or in the Future?

	Yes	No
1. Can you work alone easily and effectively day after day without having to socialize with other people?	_____	_____
2. Can you present yourself, your product, or your service confidently and enthusiastically so that a listener can comprehend not only your presentation but also the benefits he or she would derive from it?	_____	_____
3. Can you manage time effectively? To a self-employed person, that means you are able and willing to sort out priorities from the mundane and disagreeable tasks and complete them by scheduled dates.	_____	_____
4. Can you commit yourself to working long hours, sometimes 6 or 7 days a week, knowing that you will probably have to give up other activities, and not knowing how much profit you will make, if any?	_____	_____
5. Do you like to psyche yourself up to go out and contact strangers every day to sell yourself, your product, or your service?	_____	_____
6. Can you handle repeated rejections without becoming despondent and giving up?	_____	_____
7. Can you pick yourself up after a major defeat and move ahead?	_____	_____
8. Can you write convincing and persuasive business letters that show the reader you are a professional businessperson?	_____	_____
9. Can you confidently quote your hourly, daily, project, or retainer fee without fearing that your customer or client will reject you?	_____	_____
10. Can you live with the knowledge that each day you are "winging it" and may face days, weeks, and months knowing that your creditors will be contacting you for money you may owe them?	_____	_____
11. Can you live with a high profile of ongoing frustrations, incompletions, and uncertainties that often are a part of the process of producing results?	_____	_____
12. Can you handle money practically, accurately, and with a regard for keeping thorough financial records and putting money away for rainy days?	_____	_____

	Yes	No
13. Can you set measurable objectives and accomplish them by specified dates?	_____	_____
14. Can you be flexible and recognize that you, your product, or your service may have to be revised, repackaged, refinanced, or updated to compete with similar or better products or services?	_____	_____
15. Are you willing to spend the time and money that is often required to prepare yourself to embark upon self-employment?	_____	_____
16. Can you tell people what you are offering, what you want, and ask for the sale?	_____	_____
17. Can you concentrate with equal emphasis on not only what you are selling but on what your customer or client is buying?	_____	_____
18. Do you have the knowledge, experience, skills, and credentials that people will pay for?	_____	_____
19. Can you say that you love being self-employed, in spite of the long hours, frustrations, or erratic income, and the other problems that accompany it?	_____	_____

Using the "Right Tools" for Self-Advancement

Many talented technicians and managers today want higher, better-paying positions, but find themselves having to stand in line, pay their dues, and depend on their managers' whims and policies for promotions. Relying only on management's needs and timetable is the wrong thing to do in today's work force; in fact, waiting for management's approval can be a prescription for getting nowhere. Ambitious and talented employees need to have their own Self-Advancement Program, one they can apply to promote themselves at the right time.

Jeff, 42, is imaginative, and ambitious, and used his Self-Advancement Program to get the position he now has. A former junior accountant, he was determined to be a controller of a large corporation before he was 45. He periodically applied his Self-Advancement Program to advance himself in his profession (assistant general accountant, general accountant, manager of accounting, and controller). His present position is controller of a Fortune 500 corporation.

Jeff began by paying special attention to interviewing his bosses-to-be whenever he was being considered for a promotion or for a better position with another employer. He tried not only to make a good personal impression, but also to determine if his boss-to-be was ambitious, well qualified, and an outstanding candidate for advancement. Jeff needed to know that his boss-to-be had marketable assets, a good track record, and the quality of experience that would interest top managers in other corporations. If Jeff concluded that his boss-to-be had the required qualities, and if he liked the position or promotion being offered, he would accept the offer.

Jeff began to apply his Self-Advancement Program after he had been in his new position long enough (usually 1–3 years) to show management that he was hard-working, efficient, and capable of performing his boss's job. Next, having compiled more information about his boss, he prepared a resume describing his boss's qualifications. He then mailed the completed resume to a select number of recruiters with an unsigned note attached: "Here's a great guy. Find a top position for him."

Jeff's program succeeded. "Planning and carrying out my moves every two to three years, I marketed four bosses into better positions," he said. "Each boss always recommended me for filling his position, and management always promoted me. Now I am the controller of a Fortune 500 corporation and have a six-figure salary."

If you are striving for a better position, you'll need realistic goals—and you'll need to acquire or invent your own Self-Advancement Program. You'll need a strategy for telling the right people what you want and what you offer; more importantly, you'll need the skill to persuade them to give it to you. Your program and your communication skills will enable you to plan and make the right decisions in your best interests and at the right time.

Now is the time to get started. Begin by completing the form, "Conditions I Want to Change." Your answers will clarify your goals and help you design the program that will help you achieve them.

Conditions I Want to Change

I Want To	Yes	No
—take advantage of new opportunities in my field	_____	_____
—quit so I can enroll in a training program that will open new doors to employment and advancement	_____	_____
—quit so I can enroll in or complete a four-year college degree program	_____	_____
—quit so I can find a higher-paying position	_____	_____
—quit so I can find a position working among peers and managers whose ethics I respect	_____	_____
—quit and develop a combined career: working at two or more jobs so I can be my own boss	_____	_____
—quit to accept a position offering training in management skills	_____	_____
—quit to find a management position	_____	_____
—quit to find a position offering technical training so I can qualify for a technical management position in a few years	_____	_____
—quit to find a more challenging and financially rewarding position	_____	_____
—quit to escape from my present industry or profession	_____	_____
—quit to escape from the rumors of downsizing, mergers, and acquisitions	_____	_____
—quit because I can't get along with my peers, managers, or both	_____	_____
—quit because my boss is near my age, in good health, and I see little opportunity for me to advance or to replace him or her	_____	_____
—quit to accept an offer of employment from another company	_____	_____
—quit to obtain employment that will enable me to travel more	_____	_____
—quit to obtain employment that will enable me to travel less	_____	_____
—quit for personal health reasons, or for health reasons related to members of my family	_____	_____
—quit to relocate to another part of the country	_____	_____

I Want To	Yes	No
—quit to find employment with an organization that has stated growth objectives and can provide evidence that it is achieving at least some of them	_____	_____
—quit to accept an attractive early retirement package	_____	_____
—quit instead of accepting a position with my present employer who is relocating to another area of the country	_____	_____
—quit to accept a position with my former boss who is now a manager with another organization	_____	_____
—quit to escape the gossip, rumors, and mismanagement that prevails where I now work	_____	_____
—quit to escape a dead-end job	_____	_____
—quit to get a job with a high-tech company where I can be part of a team involved in "cutting edge" experiments and technology	_____	_____
—quit to relocate to my home town	_____	_____
—quit to take a long-planned trip	_____	_____
—quit to reduce the long daily commute from my home to my workplace	_____	_____
—quit to find employment that requires fewer hours per day and offers a four-day week, or flextime, or both	_____	_____
—quit to find a more secure position, a good retirement program, and medical benefits	_____	_____

Other Major Changes I Would Like to Make: _____

_____

_____

_____

Some May Never Say "Now" Is the Right Time

Some people take initial steps to make major changes in their life and work, but never get beyond the initial steps. They are not ready, willing, or interested in undertaking the necessary hard work to make major changes. Sadly, they give up; they tolerate their boring, repetitive, dead-end job and wait for their manager to promote them. These people never experience the intense satisfaction that comes from having achieved an important objective.

Fran, 28, may never say "now" is the right time. "Nine years ago, I started to work as a federal government clerk," she said. "Now I've advanced to Accountant II: a boring, routine job. My supervisor suggests I take the examination for Accountant I, but I won't take it. I'm not interested in another boring job.

"I could never leave my job with the government for profit-making companies or nonprofit organizations. I've always followed my late father's advice that government employment is interesting and secure. He said that if I got a good government job, I should keep it because I'll never have to leave it. I'm doing—and will continue to do—just what he told me to do."

If you have taken initial steps on your pathway to making major changes, take your next step by completing the form "Puritans and Pilgrims. Your answers will help you sum up how you respond to problems and challenges in your life and work. Be honest with yourself—decide whether you are conservative, dependent, and reactive (a puritan), or progressive, independent, and proactive (a pilgrim). Your answers will help you decide whether or not you can make the major changes you want to make.

"Puritans"

I Am

—serious and dedicated
—hardworking and dependable
—a defender of the status quo
—a risk avoider
—resolved to keep my complaints and disappointments to myself even when I believe I am "right" or have "good cause"
—often suffering inwardly while appearing "brave"
—always attempting to maintain a respectable facade at all costs
—convinced that management will promote me some day, but I don't have or seek evidence to support my belief
—confident that my real rewards will appear in heaven or in a future life, and all I need do now is "build up points"
—not expecting that my work will ever be much fun, and would feel "guilty" if it were fun
—confident that people who do enjoy their work are lucky and privileged; I have difficulty comprehending how they can be so lucky
—a regular depositor of small amounts of money in a savings account that pays 5% interest because it is the "safe" way and my parents did it that way. Any other way is risky and scary.
—eager to have people like me
—always insisting on knowing all the facts before I make important decisions; in fact, if I don't have all the facts, I don't make them
—convinced that people who are outgoing, happy, life-of-the-party types really are seeking a lot of attention. I'm not like them at all.
—envious of people who are successful and win prizes
—an avoider of conflict at all times; conflict makes me miserable
—certain that I deserve more acknowledgment than I get, but I don't ask for it
—a worrier
—afraid to assert my opinion because I would be challenging authority
—secretly convinced, however, that someone must be having a good time somewhere

"Pilgrims"

I

—believe in myself, my ideals, and my ability to accomplish important work, now and in the future
—have short- and long-range goals, and I am busy pursuing them
—can and do pursue goals that are not necessarily well defined when I start to pursue them
—can tell people what I offer, what I want, and what I am willing to do to get it
—can take or create risks needed to accomplish objectives that are important to me
—can and do ask friends, strangers, and peers for advice, information, contacts, or support
—try new things and develop new interests
—am open to unexpected challenges and can say "why not me?"
—know how to overcome ambivalence by doing reasonable research, or completing any reasonable action necessary to make decisions without first having all the facts
—act from my ongoing sense of purpose, not in fear of what "others" will think of me
—can celebrate my own (and others) victories
—believe I am entitled to receive some rewards, recognition, and "goodies" in my life
—convey the impression that I enjoy life, even its ups and downs
—can share my sense of humor with others
—often repeat this message: if you are going to walk on thin ice, you may as well dance!

I am predominently a _____

I am "half Puritan" and "half Pilgrim" _____

My major changes should require me to _____

Overcoming Emotional Roadblocks

All of the people we met in this chapter (Gloria, Duane, Barbara, Pat, and Jeff) overcame emotional roadblocks and succeeded in charting new personal directions and achieving new goals.

Gloria overcame her doubts about the private sector and resolved to make a major change: pursue a higher income. Duane overcame his practice of moving from one job to another without reflecting on his needs and convictions and resolved to seek employment in a community where he felt at home. Barbara and Pat overcame their hesitations about what to do next and resolved to acquire new skills so they could become self-employed. Jeff overcame his feelings of dependency on management and resolved to apply his own self-advancement program and energies until he had succeeded in achieving his present objective.

To overcome your emotional roadblocks in charting new directions or achieving new goals, begin by answering the following questions:

1. What do I really want to change about my life and work right now?

2. What will I need to do to make these changes?

3. What information, facts, and contacts will I need to have before I make these changes?

4. What compromises, if any, will I need to make to chart new directions or to achieve new goals?

5. Who can assist me (provide information, advice, direction, referrals, financial support) in my effort to chart new directions or to achieve new goals?

Your honest answers to these questions will help you clarify the major changes you want to make. You will also become more self-confident as you take steps to change them.

Making Major Changes in Your Own Way

Gloria, the former curriculum planner for the state of Nevada, made major changes in her career goal because she realized she needed a higher income. "I succeeded," she said, "because I learned two new skills: how to (1) research a company and develop a strategy for seeking employment, and (2) present my positive attitude and accomplishments to persuade the key representative of a major company to hire me for a position for which I had few qualifications."

Duane, the former retail store manager, made major changes in his life and career by first taking time to sit down, talk, listen to himself, and sum up feelings and convictions that he'd never articulated. "Listening to myself complain, clarifying my feelings, defining high-priority feelings and goals, and going after them, is a new experience for me," he said. "I've become a much more self-accepting person."

The couple planning on becoming self-employed, Barbara and Pat, discovered that good planning, new skills, and an appropriate time plan belonged on their list of major changes to make. "I learned there is a right time, a not-so-right time, and a wrong time to make major changes," said Pat. "Taking time to prepare ourselves was the best thing we did."

Jeff advanced his career from junior accountant to controller because he learned that career advancement sometimes required an ambitious person to play the "game" of self-promotion. "Each time I played the game, I was able to open doors and felt I was making important choices, my choices, not waiting for management to make them for me."

How Do High Achievers Do It?

Individuals who have worked at the same job or in the same profession for a long time, frequently become dissatisfied because their present work situation no longer offers them rewards and satisfaction. Some of them fall back on outdated values and attitudes such as "do nothing; wait and see what happens" or "management will take care of you." Still others begin to focus outward while searching for a new job or career. These are not the right steps to take for seeking ways to revitalize, redirect, or change a stalled job or career.

Looking Inward and Defining New Goals

The first step toward establishing external pathways to reach external goals is to focus on what you would like to do that will be better than whatever you are doing now.

You should determine which factors about your work must change to make your work better. So, look inward. Sum up the needs you want met, interests you want to pursue, and values you want to act on.

Next, list rewards and satisfactions you'd like to receive from your work. Then, list the specific changes you would like to make in your life and work. To accomplish these goals, allow yourself time for an inward dialogue with yourself. Often, this dialogue becomes both the cause and source of new insights that serve as your guiding beacon. New personal insights spark different actions that enable you to create the rewards and satisfactions you want now. Maintain your dialogue; if you do, it will be easier for you to establish and pursue external pathways to reach external goals. Last, request assistance from others, especially friends who can listen and offer suggestions, support, and constructive criticisms.

George, 36, a vice-president of a human resources department in Los Angeles, is a good example of what can happen to anyone who doesn't first take time to look inward and define new goals. He is stuck in a dead-end job. "Since 1984, I have worked at the same job for a major insurance company. In 1989, I began to feel that I was treadmilling my way through a sea of never-challenging work into a never-changing future. So, I decided to look for another similar position with a new company. I mailed 600 resumes to major corporations nationwide, but paid no attention to summing up new areas of expertise that I wanted to learn, or to progressive companies to contact. The results were a disaster—I received only ten negative responses, no telephone calls, and no interviews. After six months, I gave up my search. Now I'm depressed, and have resigned myself to staying where I am."

George has joined the ranks of employed American workers who surrender to the lack of challenge, rewards, and satisfaction in their present job. What happened to George can happen to anyone who neglects to define goals, including the companies and professions where these goals may be achieved.

The purpose of this chapter is to get you started on your pathway of defining goals when you change, revitalize, or redirect your career. To help you advance, some of my clients will describe how they looked inward and identified needs, interests, and goals.

Some clients looked inwardly and quickly realize they wanted out of their present position and into a better one in another organization.

Roberta, 42, a recently divorced homemaker, returned

to work after a 15-year absence. "After my divorce, I used my savings to buy a franchise: a retail ice cream store. After six months of 16-hour days, I knew I couldn't produce a profit and would have to sell it. I asked myself what I should do next," she said.

When Roberta decided to first look inward on her own feelings and beliefs, she got in touch with her personal needs, interests, and values that really were important to her. Below is a summary of her recent work experience:

Working with people: included researching, buying, organizing, managing employees, waiting on customers, communicating with bankers, suppliers, real estate agents, and scheduling

Working with data: included designing and maintaining records, preparing payroll, tax forms, and filing

Working with things: included shopping for, installing, cleaning, painting, and maintaining things

Roberta quickly realized she needed to work with people in a business-oriented environment; it was interesting and exciting. She didn't mind working with data, but didn't want to do it all the time. She completed her summary by answering the questions on the forms, "Look Inward: My First Step Toward Defining Goals" and "Factors I Want to Change." Her answers on the "Look Inward" form showed that she wants to improve her standard of living and lifestyle; maintain secure and stable employment; exercise a high degree of independence, freedom, authority, and responsibility; and develop her intellectual, technical, and creative skills. Her answers on the "Factors I Want to Change" form show that she really wants a full-time job; an acceptable round-trip daily commute; a company or organization large enough to offer her opportunities for advancement; in-house training programs; an opportunity to work among peers, associates, and friends; and prospects for salary increases. Combined, Roberta's conclusions became her new goals.

Roberta was realistic, ambitious, and energetic. She could have related her skills and needs to any one of several jobs or careers—restaurant manager, retail store manager, retail food checker, among others—but she decided to apply for employment in a bank because it was large and complex and could offer the opportunities she was now seeking. She prepared a brief resume showing her experience and strengths. Soon, after having contacted managers in several banks, she obtained a position as a teller trainee at a local branch bank. That was three years ago. Now, after four promotions, Roberta is the branch manager of an expanding suburban bank. Roberta's success demonstrates the importance of first looking inward: her decisions helped her find a position she wanted and select the right kind of opportunity that were available. "Accepting employment in a large organization was my best decision," she recently said.

To get herself started, Roberta completed a personal summary, which appears at the end of this chapter. There are many ways to jumpstart a stalled career; writing down your true feelings at crisis points is one of them. The summary helped Roberta get started—yours can help you get started too.

If you want to change from one kind of work environment to another, begin by looking inward. Sum up your needs, interests, and values. Be specific: tell yourself whether, how, and why you want to work with people, with data, and with things. Your answers will contribute to your shaping of the goals you want to pursue. Also, completing the forms in this chapter will produce many benefits and rewards in the form of self-confidence as you find or create the work you want to do.

Roberta's Summary

Look Inward: My First Step Toward Defining Goals that Will Jumpstart My Stalled Job or Career

My goals for my life and work, and the percentage of importance I attach to each one at this time, appear under Column I. My list is not intended to be all inclusive, nor are the topics in a suggested order of importance. In contrast, my opportunities to meet my needs and express my interests and values in my present job or career appear under Column II. My goals—reported in percentages under Column I—total 100%. My opportunities for satisfaction reported in percentages under Column II do not need or show a total figure.

	I % Points (0–100)	II % Opportunity to Satisfy (0–100)
1. Work for a nonprofit organization that provides education programs and/or services to benefit the general public	0	0
2. Develop rewarding relationships among a wide range of coworkers, associates, and friends	15	5
3. Improve my standard of living and lifestyle	20	0
4. Maintain secure, stable employment	20	0
5. Exercise a high degree of independence, freedom, authority, and responsibility to achieve stated objectives	15	0
6. Become financially independent	5	0
7. Compete with coworkers, peers, and associates to achieve financial rewards, recognition, and status	10	0
8. Use and develop my intellectual, technical, and creative skills in my chosen field	15	0
9. Become recognized nationwide for my expertise, services, ideas, or accomplishments	0	0
10. Become self-employed in my own business or as a consultant	0	0
11. Other(s) _____		
_____	0	0
	_____*	

*Must = 100%

Roberta's Summary

Factors I Want to Change The factors about my life and work I want to improve, revise, or eliminate that would make my career more interesting, valuable, and rewarding:

	Acceptable	Want to Change
1. Role and importance of work in my life		X
Changes I'd like to make:		
—to support an attractive lifestyle		
—as an end in itself—source of personal identity, high financial rewards, status, power, and visibility		
—more time to myself		X
—a full-time position	X	X
—other _____		
2. Geographical location of my work		
Changes I'd like to make:		

<u>X</u> local   __ another state

__ elsewhere in the state   __ overseas

	Acceptable	Want to Change
3. Round-trip daily commute to/from my work		
Changes I'd like to make:		
25–50 miles to/from home	X	

__ distance?   __ method?

__ frequency?   __ work at home

	Acceptable	Want to Change
4. Hours of overtime		
__ expected?		
__ scheduled?		
<u>X</u> none		X
5. Industry or profession		
Changes I'd like to make:		

__ expanding   __ market-driven

__ stable   __ nonprofit

__ contracting   <u>X</u> profit

__ service-dedicated   __ technology-driven

	Acceptable	Want to Change

6. Company or organization

   Changes I'd like to make:

   ___ headquartered where?

   ___ ownership?

   ___ purpose or mission statement?

   ___ management style?

   ___ size?

   ___ product or product line?

   ___ reputation in its industry?

   ___ reputation in the local community?

7. Environment I work in

   Changes I'd like to make:

   ___ professional/technical competence of cowor-kers and management

   ___ professional ethics of coworkers and man-agement

   ___ employees recognize my talents and abili-ties, and I respect theirs

   X opportunity to participate in in-house training programs

   X good prospects for financial and career ad-vancement

8. Opportunity to play a proactive role in resolving daily problems, issues, and challenges, and to contribute to short- and long-term organization plans and goals   X

9. Opportunity to maintain and/or develop ever-changing state-of-the-art knowledge, abilities, and skills by cross-training or company-financed continuing education programs

10. Other(s) _____

Becoming a Consultant

Some clients look inward and conclude that now they're ready to be a consultant.

Warren, 48, is an executive who looked inward and concluded that he was ready, qualified, and most important motivated to become a consultant. "After having been told many times that I was overqualified and that my salary expectations were too high, I decided to take a good look at myself," he said. "Completing the forms-especially "The Role of the Consultant: Is it for Me?"—really helped me realize what I want to do and what personal and financial satisfactions I want from my work. I thought a long time about the questions in the consultant form and concluded that I'm ready to be a consultant. Now, one year later, I have company clients locally and nationwide. Becoming a consultant is the best decision I've made in years."

If you are interested in becoming a consultant, begin by looking inward and ask yourself if you are qualified and willing to work the way consultants work. Your answers will help you act on what is really important to you. To get started, review Warren's completed forms on the next few pages. Next, complete the blank copies of these same forms at the end of this chapter. Your answers will help you decide if you have the experience, skills, and self-discipline required to become a consultant. Your answers will improve your self-confidence and belief that you can succeed in the consulting profession.

Warren's Summary

Look Inward: My First Step Toward Defining Goals That Will Jumpstart My Stalled Job or Career

My goals for my life and work, and the percentage of importance I attach to each one at this time, appear under Column I. My list is not intended to be all inclusive, nor are the topics in a suggested order of importance. In contrast, my opportunities to meet my needs and express my interests and values in my present job or career appear under Column II. My goals—reported in percentages under Column I—total 100%. My opportunities for satisfaction reported in percentages under Column II do not need or show a total figure.

	I % Points (0–100)	II % Opportunity to satisfy (0–100)
1. Work for a nonprofit organization that provides education programs and/or services to benefit the general public	0	0
2. Develop rewarding relationships among a wide range of coworkers, associates, and friends	5	15
3. Improve my standard of living and lifestyle	5	5
4. Maintain secure, stable employment	5	10
5. Exercise a high degree of independence, freedom, authority, and responsibility to achieve stated objectives	18	10
6. Become financially independent	13	5
7. Compete with coworkers, peers, and associates to achieve financial rewards, recognition, and status	18	5
8. Use and develop my intellectual, technical, and creative skills in my chosen field	18	10
9. Become recognized nationwide for my expertise, services, ideas, or accomplishments	10	5
10. Become self-employed in my own business or as a consultant	10	0
11. Other(s) _____		
_____		
	100% *	

*Must = 100%

Warren's Summary

Factors I Want to Change The factors about my life and work I want to improve, revise, or eliminate that would make my career more interesting, valuable, and rewarding:

	Acceptable	Want to Change
1. Role and importance of work in my life		X
Changes I'd like to make:		
—to support an attractive lifestyle		
—as an end in itself—source of personal identity, high financial rewards, status, power, and visibility	X	
—more time to myself		
—a full-time position		
—other <u>want to work nationwide</u>	X	
2. Geographical location of my work		
Changes I'd like to make:		
__ local __ another state		
__ elsewhere in the state __ overseas		
3. Round-trip daily commute to/from my work		
Changes I'd like to make:		
<u>Willing to travel extensively</u>	X	
__ distance? __ method?		
__ frequency? __ work at home		
4. Hours of overtime		
__ expected?		
__ scheduled?		
__ none		
__ as required	X	
5. Industry or profession		
Changes I'd like to make:		
__ expanding __ market-driven		
__ stable __ nonprofit		
__ contracting __ profit		
__ service-dedicated __ technology-driven		

	<u>Acceptable</u>	<u>Want to Change</u>

6. Company or organization

   Changes I'd like to make:

   ___ headquartered where?

   ___ ownership?

   ___ purpose or mission statement?

   ___ management style?

   ___ size?

   ___ product or product line?

   ___ reputation in its industry?

   ___ reputation in the local community?   _____   _____

7. Environment I work in

   Changes I'd like to make:

   ___ professional/technical competence of coworkers and management

   ___ professional ethics of coworkers and management

   <u>X</u> employees recognize my talents and abilities, and I respect theirs

   ___ opportunity to participate in in-house training
   programs

   ___ good prospects for financial and career advancement   _____   _____

8. Opportunity to play a proactive role in resolving
   daily problems, issues, and challenges, and to
   contribute to short- and long-term organization
   plans and goals   _____   _____

9. Opportunity to maintain and/or develop ever-
   changing state-of-the-art knowledge, abilities,
   and skills by cross-training or company-financed
   continuing education programs   _____   _____

10. Other(s) <u>Willing to travel_____</u>   ___X___   _____

Warren's Summary

The Role of the Consultant: Is it for Me?

	Yes	No
1. Do I like to research, write, and present reports about trends, conditions, and results often required to conduct business operations?	X	
2. When required to undertake and complete assignments, such as the ones listed above, do I prefer to work alone or as a member of a group?	X	
3. Do I feel competent to lead a group dedicated to summing up and presenting conclusions about a problem to be solved, and to recommend and promote solutions for that problem?	X	
4. Do I feel competent when required to write numerous statistical/technical reports for discussion and action by general and technical managers?	X	
5. Can I work alone for hours, days, and weeks without taking time off?	X	
6. Can I commit myself to invest up to 60% of my time marketing my services to prospective clients and not become dejected and quit as a result of frequent rejections?	X	
7. Do I live with unpredictable income?	X	
8. Can I prepare a realistic business plan that shows my short- and long-term objectives, methods for achieving them, and projected costs for at least the first two years of my consulting business?	X	
9. Can I easily and comfortably "close" a sales presentation for a new or present client?	X	
10. Can I easily quote rates and payment terms that reveal to clients my sense of worth as well as my knowledge of prevailing rates often paid by clients for my kind of service?	X	

Protecting the Status Quo

When some people look inward, they decide their midlife goal is to protect their present salary, pension rights, and medical coverage. As a result, they may accept a different position with their present employer.

Claire, 48, a senior flight attendant for 25 years, chose to protect her long-time benefits accrued from her present employer. "Six months ago, I injured my shoulder while on a flight to Honolulu," she said. "At first I panicked, afraid that management would lay me off because I could no longer lift heavy luggage. I took a leave of absence and got a job as a sales trainee with an insurance company."

Claire made major changes without first looking inward and concluding what she needed to do, what interested her, and what alternatives she had with the airline. "I just overlooked the fact that if I quit my job, I'd reduce my pension rights, medical coverage for my injury, and my present high salary. I wasn't thinking clearly."

After a few months as a sales trainee, Claire began to look inward. Her manager told her that her performance and sales skills were not sufficiently aggressive, that she didn't meet their high standards, and that they would not offer her medical coverage for her shoulder injury. At this point, Claire realized that she couldn't afford to change her career and had to protect the benefits she had built up. So, she looked for jobs she could do on the ground at her same salary with her present employer—she found one and accepted it.

Claire is a good example of a person who was *forced* to look inward. She had been reacting to fear of what the airline managers would do, not from what she recognized as necessary, interesting, and valuable for her. "Even though my new job on the ground isn't as interesting, I am confident that I've made the right decision," she said.

If you need to make major changes in your work due to health or financial circumstances, take time to assess your real situation before you make those changes. You'll discover that making only minor changes can change your point of view about life and the satisfactions you derive from your work.

Succumbing to "Career Death"

Some clients remain stalled in their career path at critical stages even though their present position no longer meets their needs.

Larry, 38, assistant vice-president, product development, for a major consumer products company, remained stalled in his career path. "For five years I was the golden-haired 'up and comer' in my company," he said. "But after four promotions, I suddenly fell out of favor with my boss. He didn't say so, I didn't seek clarification, but it happened. Now I no longer work so hard, and I've joined the other 'discarded executives' still employed in our company."

What happened to Larry can happen to anyone. How you interpret these events and act on them will determine if you will continue to move ahead or suffer "career death." But Larry not only gave up, he also describes how he did it. "I began to see that another boss now had my boss's ear," he said. "He got the best assignments. I was given staff jobs, fixing unimportant problems, but my results, even the good ones, got no acknowledgments. So, I'm stuck. I guess I can hang on indefinitely. My future has peaked with the company. I know it—everyone knows it. Inside, I'm hurt, but I don't say anything to anybody."

If you are stalled in your career as a result of similar circumstances, don't believe it—you *can* jumpstart your career. Take a firm hold of your feelings in a special way. Redirect them toward finding solutions, not being mired in problems. Be honest with yourself—start writing down honest summaries of your strengths, knowledge, victories, and what you've learned from your defeats. Keep updating your summary. Soon you're bound to see an inventory of your marketable assets that will encourage you to act proactively.

Roberta, Warren, and Claire succeeded in looking inward, summing up important conclusions and goals, and acting on them in their own best interests at the right time. You can too!

My Summary

Look Inward: My First Step Toward Defining Goals that Will Jumpstart My Stalled Job or Career

My goals for my life and work, and the percentage of importance I attach to each one at this time, appear under Column I. My list is not intended to be all inclusive, nor are the topics in a suggested order of importance. In contrast, my opportunities to meet my needs and express my interests and values in my present job or career appear under Column II. My goals—reported in percentages under Column I—total 100%. My opportunities for satisfaction reported in percentages under Column II do not need or show a total figure.

	I % Points (0–100)	II % Opportunity to satisfy (0–100)
1. Work for a nonprofit organization that provides education programs and/or services to benefit the general public	_____	_____
2. Develop rewarding relationships among a wide range of coworkers, associates, and friends	_____	_____
3. Improve my standard of living and lifestyle	_____	_____
4. Maintain secure, stable employment	_____	_____
5. Exercise a high degree of independence, freedom, authority, and responsibility to achieve stated objectives	_____	_____
6. Become financially independent	_____	_____
7. Compete with coworkers, peers, and associates to achieve financial rewards, recognition, and status	_____	_____
8. Use and develop my intellectual, technical, and creative skills in my chosen field	_____	_____
9. Become recognized nationwide for my expertise, services, ideas, or accomplishments	_____	_____
10. Become self-employed in my own business or as a consultant	_____	_____
11. Other(s) _____		
_____	_____	_____
	_____*	

*Must = 100%

My Summary

Factors I Want to Change The factors about my life and work I want to improve, revise, or eliminate that would make my career more interesting, valuable, and rewarding:

	Acceptable	Want to Change
1. Role and importance of work in my life	_____	_____
Changes I'd like to make:		
—to support an attractive lifestyle	_____	_____
—as an end in itself—source of personal identity, high financial rewards, status, power, and visibility	_____	_____
—more time to myself	_____	_____
—a full-time position	_____	_____
—other _____		
2. Geographical location of my work	_____	_____

Changes I'd like to make:

__ local   __ another state

__ elsewhere in the state   __ overseas

3. Round-trip daily commute to/from my work	_____	_____
Changes I'd like to make:		
_____	_____	_____

__ distance?   __ method?

__ frequency? __ work at home	_____	_____
4. Hours of overtime		
__ expected?	_____	_____
__ scheduled?	_____	_____
__ none	_____	_____
5. Industry or profession		
Changes I'd like to make:	_____	_____

__ expanding   __ market-driven

__ stable   __ nonprofit

__ contracting   __ profit

__ service-dedicated   __ technology-driven

	Acceptable	Want to Change

6. Company or organization

   Changes I'd like to make:

   ___ headquartered where?

   ___ ownership?

   ___ purpose or mission statement?

   ___ management style?

   ___ size?

   ___ product or product line?

   ___ reputation in its industry?

   ___ reputation in the local community?

	_____	_____

7. Environment I work in

   Changes I'd like to make:

   ___ professional/technical competence of cowor-kers and management

   ___ professional ethics of coworkers and man-agement

   ___ employees recognize my talents and abili-ties, and I respect theirs

   ___ opportunity to participate in in-house training programs

   ___ good prospects for financial and career ad-vancement

	_____	_____

8. Opportunity to play a proactive role in resolving daily problems, issues, and challenges, and to contribute to short- and long-term organization plans and goals

	_____	_____

9. Opportunity to maintain and/or develop ever-changing state-of-the-art knowledge, abilities, and skills by cross-training or company-financed continuing education programs

	_____	_____

10. Other(s) _____

	_____	_____

My Summary

The Role of the Consultant: Is it for Me?

	Yes	No

1. Do I like to research, write, and present reports about trends, conditions, and results often required to conduct business operations?

2. When required to undertake and complete assignments, such as the ones listed above, do I prefer to work alone or as a member of a group?

3. Do I feel competent to lead a group dedicated to summing up and presenting conclusions about a problem to be solved, and to recommend and promote solutions for that problem?

4. Do I feel competent when required to write numerous statistical/technical reports for discussion and action by general and technical managers?

5. Can I work alone for hours, days, and weeks without taking time off?

6. Can I commit myself to invest up to 60% of my time marketing my services to prospective clients and not become dejected and quit as a result of frequent rejections?

7. Do I live with unpredictable income?

8. Can I prepare a realistic business plan that shows my short- and long-term objectives, methods for achieving them, and projected costs for at least the first two years of my consulting business?

9. Can I easily and comfortably "close" a sales presentation for a new or present client?

10. Can I easily quote rates and payment terms that reveal to clients my sense of worth as well as my knowledge of prevailing rates often paid by clients for my kind of service?

Roberta's Personal Summary

I Am	a long-time resident of "x" town and the former owner and manager of "y" store located at "z" address.
I Can	plan, organize, and act as a working supervisor or manager. For three years, I performed as both supervisor and manager: investigated and purchased the franchise, leased retail space, installed equipment, established a credit line with a local bank; hired, trained, supervised 1–25 part- and full-time employees, handled payroll, paid taxes, wrote advertising copy, and waited on customers. Sold the store in June, 1988.
I Want	information about job openings and/or career opportunities in your organization. Resume available upon request.
I Offer	more than three years of retail management experience, a wide range of contacts with members of the community, and a positive attitude. I am goal-directed, results-oriented, and a problem solver.
I Am Willing to	start in any position that will enable me to apply my business experience, and look forward to career and financial advancement.

My Other Strengths Include:

_____

_____

_____

_____

Personal Summary

Step I: Summing Up: Reflections on my present job or career situation, and my interpretations of them.

_____

_____

_____

_____

Step II: Taking Stock: Knowledge, experience, abilities, and skills acquired. Emphasis is on the areas I want to learn, develop, or apply NOW.

_____

_____

_____

_____

Step III: Changes I would like to make that would make my present or another job or career "ideal":

_____

_____

_____

_____

Step IV: Compromises I Am Willing to Accept to Find or Create My "Ideal" Job or Career:

_____

_____

_____

_____

Step V: My Plan for Finding or Creating the Job or Career that I Want Now or at the Right Time:

_____

_____

_____

_____

Do What Successful People Do

Early in my years as a career consultant, I emphasized the importance of my clients developing constructive and supportive relationships with key people in their lives. Such relationships can help them jumpstart their jobs or careers in many and unexpected ways. Some of my clients had often taken only a few steps in this direction, and sometimes, none at all. Those who are at a critical stage in their career will frequently try to resolve the crisis by working alone—often for a long time—to move beyond it. They think they should be able to make major changes without assistance from others. Some, not making much progress in finding solutions, will pretend they are satisfied with their present career even though it no longer interests them. Others, who did not receive a promised promotion, will refuse to admit that they have peaked in their career. Some are victims of the "golden handcuffs" (high salaries, generous benefits, automatic salary increases, etc.), and will suffer from boredom rather than break the "handcuffs" and seek new opportunities.

Whether working alone, resolving career problems by ignoring them, or making the best of boredom and the lack of opportunities, all of these are wrong steps to take for those who seek new career opportunities and challenges in the 1990s.

Gail, 32, a former sales representative for a major food products manufacturer, tried to solve her problems without support, advice, constructive suggestions, or job referrals from friends or others who could help her. As a result, she was depressed, bitter, and doing nothing to seek assistance or find employment.

"Since 1987, I had surpassed my sales quota and each year received a bonus," Gail said. "In January 1989, my boss hired his son right out of college. I could see my boss was training his son to take my job, but I didn't seek another position. Instead, I shoved my anxieties aside. Soon, my boss divided my territory in half and gave 56 of my retail clients to his son. Last month, my boss laid me off—he said I was not meeting my sales quota."

Gail's story illustrates the plight of many employees who, alone in times of serious need, often lack a community of people to turn to for help. They also lack a strategy for initiating contacts with the "right" people and for gaining their support in a way that will provide "bridges" to other employment or career opportunities.

Looking Outward and Developing Key Contacts

In my practice, I show my clients how to organize and apply their strategy and skills to contact people who can help them. I call it a "People Management Program." Everyone trying to resolve a work or career crisis can benefit from applying such a program. Clients who have successfully applied the strategies and tools in their programs have discovered that it produces many benefits, leads, and information not easily available in the highly specialized, ever-restructuring work force of the 1990s.

In my instructions, I show clients how to develop their own records of people who can and will help them. We select people in three areas: (1) peers, supervisors, and managers in their present organization or career field; (2) friends, peers, and associates outside their organization or career field; and (3) strangers who are or may be willing to assist them.

We select people for their program only if they meet the

following criteria: they are good listeners; trustworthy; and sources of good advice, support, constructive criticism, and/or referrals to key persons who know of job openings or opportunities. We are especially interested in opportunity seekers, opinion makers, movers, and shakers. We also select people who are at least familiar with the level of work the client does or might want to do, and are willing to act on his or her behalf. Such criteria are invaluable; they also help us screen and select only those who are best equipped and willing to help at the right time.

In Chapter 5, you will learn to organize and apply your own "People Management Program." You can then decide whether to apply it in areas (1), (2), and/or (3). Each day, you will apply Winston Churchill's credo "actions today" and you will initiate or expand your contacts with key persons. Each person you include in your program will help you resolve your life or career crisis. You are always in charge of your own program and responsible for its success. The program helps you to be effective, self-directing, self-managing, self-accountable, self-developing, and self-promoting.

Advancing Your Career Through a People Management Program

Some people quickly learn and apply their people management program to advance their careers.

Howard, 28, a recent college graduate working for a major CPA firm, used his "People Management Program" to accelerate his prospects for advancement. He expressed an interest in obtaining a "blueprint"—or guidelines—that would help him learn how to conduct himself professionally among more experienced workers. "I want to improve my communication skills, become a team member, and be respected for my technical competence," he said. His program—suggestions that can benefit anyone working in a large office—enabled him to accomplish his objectives, "I periodically evaluated my attitudes and accomplishments, recorded areas for self-improvement, and I think I am doing well when it comes to attracting my manager's attention," he said.

Howard's program enabled him to avoid making two of the most common errors made by career seekers: (1) going overboard in the belief that self-advancement is determined by knowing the "right" people, overlooking the equal importance of technical competence, or the opposite; and (2) dedicating themselves to acquiring technical competence—often working alone long hours—in the mistaken belief that their dedication and commitment will be recognized and rewarded, overlooking the equal importance of communicating and working well with fellow employees at all levels.

Howard's program enabled him to keep in perspective the importance of improving both his people management skills and his technical competence. As a result, it seems safe to assume that Howard will be able to steer his career upward and avoid having to jumpstart his career pathway in the years ahead.

If you believe you will benefit from having your own "People Management Program," begin by reviewing the topics in Howard's program below. From the list of recommendations, select the ones you should remember and practice. Select others that are more specifically related to your present job and to the factors that are important for advancement. Evaluate your performance under "Comments" and pursue a corrective course of action to make the changes you've entered under "Need Improvement." Like Howard, you may feel more confident about managing your career and developing attitudes and skills that can help you jumpstart your career now.

Howard's People Management Program

I Plan To	Comments	Need Improvement
Cultivate and maintain good communication	_____	_____
Anticipate and meet my boss's needs and make him or her look good with his or her superiors. I'll also look for evidence that my boss is looking out for my best interests and career development	_____	_____
Show my constructive "can do" attitude and concern for achieving stated objectives	_____	_____
Accept tasks or assignments that help expand my knowledge, abilities, and skills in such areas as communications, product knowledge, service skills, and/or technology	_____	_____
Demonstrate my interest in the company, or in my field, by investing my own time and money to improve my knowledge and skills. If appropriate, I plan to inform my boss after I have successfully completed technical or formal education courses	_____	_____
Practice win-win communication skills when negotiating solutions with coworkers or the public	_____	_____
Temper the pursuit of my ego needs with regard for personal honesty and pursuit of truth, whether for myself, the company, or on behalf of others	_____	_____
Speak up, ask for promotions that will advance my career, reinforce my request with work-related data, reports, results, success stories that demonstrate I am the best person for the position	_____	_____
Share my sense of humor with others	_____	_____
Remain open to the unexpected: to "messengers" I respect, whether strangers or friends, who might offer me opportunities I might not have thought possible	_____	_____
Now and again set aside a quiet moment to be by myself; I'll ask myself if the work I am doing is really important and enjoyable for me and leading me in the pathway I want to follow	_____	_____
Remember that every job has a beginning, midpoint, and an end; success comes to those who move ahead to accomplish more worthy goals	_____	_____

Breaking Out of Your Present Career

Some people need a "People Management Program" that will help them break out of their present organization and/ or career and explore other career options.

Melissa, 34, an office manager for a large retailer, wanted not only to break out of this job, but out of the retail field as well. She admitted her lack of experience and skills in investigating other kinds of work. "When I started to look for other kinds of work, I was scared. I had to overcome my reluctance to ask questions of friends or strangers. The first time I tried it, I thought I was drowning."

Pursuing alternative jobs or careers requires having a unique set of personal qualities: courage, resolve, commitment to risk taking, communication skills, and perseverance. Some people explore other jobs or careers easily; others need tutoring, practice, and more awareness of what you—the communicator—must do to be successful. The form, "Proactive Communication" provides insight into the dynamics of communicating with friends and/or strangers.

You may hesitate to tell people that you are planning to change your job or career. You may not feel confident or skillful doing it, but practice will improve your performance. Being able to speak easily and comfortably about your needs and wants is a necessary—even indispensable—skill. To help my clients take hold and direct the required personal energy and purpose to get started, I show them the chart, "Proactive Communication" form. The more they practice, the sooner they see the importance of speaking enthusiastically about their plan and progress in making major personal changes. Enthusiasm and self-confidence are powerful forces: they attract people to you. So, practice proactive communication. Melissa stated it best: "Interviewing the people I had screened and selected did more for my self-confidence and self-esteem than anything I'd done for myself in the last five years."

Proactive Communication

Actions	Results
Acting positively to produce a constructive solution	*Enthusiasm* about your ever-growing skill and success in gathering information and pursuing new goals—sometimes acting without first having in hand all the information you want and need
Willing to act to produce a realistic result	*Increased Self-Confidence* from your ever-increasing skills in selecting and asking questions and in receiving useful answers from friends and strangers
Wishing for a successful solution	*Increased Self-Acceptance* of your new skills in telling strangers or friends what you want, what you offer, what benefits you can produce, and asking them for information and/or assistance
Giving yourself permission	*Self-Doubt/Ambivalence* Feelings: 'I can never do it,' 'Who me?', 'some day, but not now,' are strong and 'escape or avoidance' is my way out
Suppressing your anxieties	*Confusion/Uncertainty* Feelings: 'It's hard to hear the problem described if it's my problem or if I'm involved in it; too much to think about; better not think about it at all'

Selecting Key Contacts You may need help in selecting the "right" people to contact, knowing what to say to them, and how to say it. When developing a "People Management Program," looking outward and requesting information and/or assistance from key people is a skill necessary to discovering alternative occupations or careers. Of equal importance is gathering information from all kinds of people and learning more about the occupations and careers in the 1990s. This type of investigative interviewing improves your self-confidence and is likely to result in successful interviews with prospective employers.

If you are actively looking outward and interviewing people, begin by talking with those you already know, like, and trust. You will feel "at home" while becoming more skilled in conducting interviews of this kind.

Stephanie, 25, started by talking with fellow employees. "I told my coworkers that I needed to make adjustments in my work and would welcome their suggestions," she said. "They knew that I could no longer handle the physical stress of teaching aerobics because of a recent automobile accident. My friends told me I was great at motivating the adults in my classes and said I'd be a very good supervisor for all of the aerobic instructors."

Stephanie believed their recommendations made a lot of sense; as a result, she jumpstarted her career by completing community college courses in effective supervision to learn more about it. Her manager, who recognized that Stephanie could no longer teach aerobics, created a new supervisor position for the eleven instructors. Looking outward, sometimes starting with people around you, opens doors to new options and support that you might not have sought.

To begin looking outward, start by stepping back and first thinking about the people you know. Select those who comprehend the kind of work you do. Select good listeners. Select people who are nonjudgmental and who give you helpful information. After each interview, write down insights, recommendations, and facts that you might want to research and use later. Ask yourself if you enjoyed the interviews. If you didn't, try to enjoy the next one. After each interview, you will experience more self-confidence and you will discover that you are becoming more skillful in conducting interviews that produce options and opportunities worth exploring.

Examples of Key People to Contact

friends _____

associates (present and former) _____

supervisors (present and former) _____

managers (present and former) _____

neighbors _____

stockbrokers _____

financial planners _____

attorneys _____

political representatives _____

instructors _____

accountants _____

certified public accountants _____

counselors _____

physicians _____

ministers _____

priests _____

members of professional associations _____

vendors who visit your company or plant _____

consultants _____

faculty advisors _____

agents _____

☐ literary _____

☐ real estate _____

☐ business _____

people you admire, don't know, but believe you'd like to talk to now _____

Gathering Information   You may need help in deciding what to say to people when you meet with them. You may have your own list of questions, or, as in Stephanie's case, you may merely want to exchange ideas and recommendations. If you prefer having a more structured list of questions, consider asking some of the following questions.

Job Title or Career Questions

- What does the person do?
- How does he or she do it?
- Where does he or she work?
- What abilities/skills does it take to succeed?
- How does one qualify for entry employment?
- Can I transfer my present or most recent experience into qualifications suitable for employment?
- What is the starting salary range?
- How does an outsider get an appointment with a key person in the company/organization?
- Your own questions:

Company/Organization Questions

- What is it like to work for this company?
  - ☐ positive reasons
  - ☐ negative reasons
- Where is the company/organization headquartered?
  - ☐ local
  - ☐ out of state
  - ☐ out of the country
- What is the company's management style?
  - ☐ authoritarian
  - ☐ participative
  - ☐ power down
  - ☐ progressive
- What is the reputation of the company in its industry?
  - ☐ major company
  - ☐ declining in performance
  - ☐ having problems
  - ☐ other
- What is the company's annual sales volume?
  - ☐ evidence of clear future goals
  - ☐ evidence of company accomplishing at least some of its goals
- Is the company people-oriented?
  - ☐ provides in-house training programs
  - ☐ promotes from within
  - ☐ has a written no-layoff policy
  - ☐ employees have high morale
  - ☐ low or high turnover
- Your own questions:

Maintaining Records   It is important for you to prepare and update records of your scheduled interviews and completed conversations, and to record dates and times for follow-ups. Use the "Contact Record" shown on page 88.

Interviewing Guidelines   Here are some guidelines to follow for setting up interviews and monitoring your progress from beginning to end:

1. Request a 15–30 minute meeting at the other person's convenience, far from telephones and interruptions.

2. Request a date and time that is mutually satisfactory.

3. Begin the meeting by explaining your plans to change your job or career.

4. Summarize your major strengths, skills, accomplishments, and any ideas you have about what you want to do next and the help you believe this person can give you.

5. If you don't know what you want to do next, say so, but add that the information you are gathering is helping you explore realistic options.

6. Listen carefully. Give each person as much eye contact as seems appropriate.

7. Speak simply. Avoid using jargon and buzz words.

8. Try to make a good impression: you may want to contact this person later for more information.

9. Speak about yourself and your present or former employer(s) in a self-accepting and constructive way.

10. Jot down notes of key points; this shows you are serious about the value of your conversation.

11. Take the initiative in ending the interview according to the time agreed upon.

12. Acknowledge the value of the interview at an appropriate time—call or send a card.

Interviewing with numerous people calls for proper record maintenance of who, where, and what was discussed. The last thing you want is confusion about who you're talking to when calls are returned. The following worksheet is a sample Contact Record which will help you maintain organization.

Contact Record

Date	Company Name Mailing Address	Phone #	Individual & Title	Reference/ Source	Contact —Date —Method	Appointment Date & Time	Grade G/M/P *	Follow-up Date

* G = Good
M = Medium
P = Poor

Refusing to Make a Change

Those who never get their "People Management Program" organized often end up working at the same boring job again and again but with different employers.

Marlene, 37, a receptionist for an established dentist, has been complaining for five years about being bored with her job. Even though she has the required education to advance in her field, she takes no steps to jumpstart her career into a more challenging and rewarding avenue. "The thought of having to meet a lot of new people, research and select other kinds of work, please new employers, and accept new responsibilities is more than I can accept right now," she said.

Only you can make the difference. Jumpstarting a career requires a willingness and determination to make major changes in your life and work. Sadly, some people cannot accept the challenge.

If you want to look outward and jumpstart your job or career with the interest and support of friends and key contact people, begin by reviewing and completing the forms in this chapter. These forms can be useful in designing a "People Management Program" that will help you accomplish personal objectives.

Create Your Ideal Job

Giving up, resigning yourself to being a mediocre employee, or quitting to accept a similar position elsewhere are major mistakes to avoid in the 1990s. If you want to find your ideal job right now, you must apply your imagination and problem-solving skills in appropriate ways and at the right time.

George, 52, a marketing representative for a producer of industrial castings, had given up. "For three years, I've been telling my regional manager that casting manufacturers in Europe and the Pacific Rim are invading our market, but he doesn't think that overseas manufacturers are a big threat," George said. "Even when I tell him our customers regard overseas castings as good as ours, and less expensive, he won't listen to me. So, I see our sales decline, soon my job will be in jeopardy, and I wait for the end to come."

George feels powerless to make marketing and pricing changes in his company's product and service, so he has given up trying to change policies, procedures, and marketing strategies.

The purpose of this chapter is to show you ways to apply your imagination, strategies, and communications skills to solve problems. This is essential in jumpstarting your job or career.

Solving a Company Problem

Introducing state-of-the-art ideas, developments, and/or technologies may jumpstart your career into an ideal position with your present employer.

Jean, 37, a national marketing manager for a major meeting and event planner, used her imagination and problem-solving skills to create her own ideal job. "Our company has been selling services to Fortune 500 company clients for 20 years," she began. "Recently our competitors have been offering our clients satellite in-house conferencing services and winning contracts we usually win. I've told my managers that our clients are showing interest in the advantages of satellite conferencing. My managers don't know anything about it, don't believe there's enough new interest to worry about it, and tell me I'm just complaining."

Jean considered the options: (1) giving up; (2) attempting to use her imagination and problem-solving skills to create her own ideal job with her present employer; or (3) quitting. She chose the second. "I located a reputable outside source of market research and analysis reports and compiled data about costs of satellite technology," she said. "I also located a reputable source of ongoing information about changing corporate trends—*The Wall Street Journal* subscription service. The market research, analysis reports, and the *WSJ* trends confirmed my belief that corporate managers are looking for cost-effective meetings and that satellite services for on-site conferences are interesting to them."

Jean had stepped back and asked herself what she and her managers could do to solve a marketing problem. She also wondered what she had to do to attract her manager's interest so he'd agree that a problem existed. "I answered both questions in my written proposal, and, for the first time, my manager really listened to me," she said. "After he'd read it, he showed it to the company president who accepted my recommendations. Now I'm invited to attend weekly management meetings to improve our company marketing strategy. I've created my own ideal job."

If you decide to create your own ideal job, begin by asking yourself what the organization's management or you can do to resolve a problem. If all parties agree that a problem exists, you may face an opportunity to solve it and be able to display your imagination and problem-solving abilities. Ask yourself questions like the ones on page 93; they will help you define and prepare verbal or written proposals. Acting in your best interests at the right time places you among the risk creators—the ones most likely to find or create their own ideal jobs in the 1990s.

	Need to Know	Need to Do	Cost (time, money, materials)	Who Will Benefit?
What can we do to improve our sales strategies/products/services/customer services?	_____	_____	_____	_____
What resources will we need?	_____	_____	_____	_____
What steps should we take to get started?	_____	_____	_____	_____
Who will be responsible for initiating and administering these changes?	_____	_____	_____	_____
What barriers are we likely to encounter?	_____	_____	_____	_____
What criteria will we apply to determine whether we accomplished the goals we resolved to accomplish?	_____	_____	_____	_____
How many days/weeks/months should we define as a satisfactory period for producing results?	_____	_____	_____	_____
Am I able to demonstrate my imagination/problem-solving skills in making these changes?	_____	_____	_____	_____
If I am successful, is my success likely to jumpstart my job/career with my present employer?	_____	_____	_____	_____

Your answers to the following questions will help you decide whether you want to jumpstart your stalled career with your present employer, seek a better position with another employer, or change your career. As a final choice, you may even decide to quit, one way of starting over.

I ask myself: **Comments**

1. What *needs* do I want met in my present
   or another job or career?   _____

   ☐ job security?

   ☐ career advancement?

   ☐ work with people I respect?

   ☐ apply my knowledge and skills?

   ☐ join a growing organization?

   ☐ other(s) _____

   _____

2. What do I want to *receive* from another job
   or career that I don't already receive?   _____

3. What challenges does my present or potential employer offer that I don't already have?   _____

4. What new or different services or products
   could I offer to my present or potential employer?   _____

5. Why would my present or potential employer be better off after using my services or products?   _____

6. What am I willing to do to rearrange my
   present job responsibilities or to find or
   create another job or career?   _____

   ☐ quit my job and accept a lower-paying
      position that offers better advance-
      ment prospects   _____

   ☐ work longer or different hours

   ☐ complete courses required to enter
      another job or career   _____

   ☐ relocate   _____

7. What knowledge, experience, skills, contacts, credentials, or tools would I most
   want to apply, learn, or develop now?   _____

8. Who might need my knowledge, expertise, skills, personality, contacts, or credentials now or in the near future?   _____

   Examples:

   _____

   _____

   _____

   _____

Solving a Personal Problem

Some people jumpstart their job or career by becoming a consultant in a shrinking industry.

Connie, 35, a former TV announcer and producer, said, "In the past 10 years, I've noted rapid changes of TV station ownership, managers, and program formats. Even worse, more and more programming is coming down from corporate headquarters, and less is local programming. It's a shrinking industry. I've concluded it cannot offer me job security or career and financial advancement."

Connie then used her imagination and problem-solving skills to find an answer for *her* problem—not, as in Jean's story, a *company* problem. "In my zeal to complete my master's degree in communications and get a TV job, I had been focusing on the needs and interests of the audience," she said. "Now that I'm in the industry, I spend more time thinking of the needs of sole proprietors, small- to medium-sized business owners, and managers who could benefit from TV, radio, and media promotion."

Connie's new direction of interest led her to complete the forms, "Self-Appraisal and Self-Inventory" and the "Business Plan" on pages 96 and 97. Now, one year later, she has more business clients than she ever imagined. "I introduce small business owners and managers to station managers, announcers, and producers; I prepare press kits, backgrounders, fact sheets, and publicity releases; and I even schedule interviews for authors with TV talk show celebrities," she said. "I created my ideal job by shifting my focus from the audiences to the business community."

You may want to leave a shrinking industry and explore ways to continue to play a role in the industry or to pursue a position in an alternative industry. Start your planning by stepping back and asking yourself what you could do that is different, what you have to offer, and what people would pay you to do.

Self-Appraisal and Self-Inventory

Good questions:

Honest answers:

1. Who *needs* (and would be willing to pay for) your knowledge, abilities, skills, and contacts?

   _____

2. What *needs* do they have that you can meet and want to meet?

   _____

3. What *services* and/or *products* could you offer clients?

   _____

4. In what way(s) would your clients benefit from using or buying your service(s) or product(s)?

   _____

5. How would you market your services and/ or products?

   _____

6. What fees would you charge your clients?

   _____

7. What terms of payments would you quote?

   _____

Connie's Business Plan

I Need: **Comments:**

A Business Identity

company name   _____

my title   _____

local address   _____

business telephone number   _____

home telephone number   _____

FAX number   _____

stationery   _____

brochures   _____

portfolio   _____

A Financial Plan

estimate of funds needed to pay start-up and
operating costs for a minimum of one year (or
more)   _____

estimate of minimum monthly income needed
to pay own salary and daily living expenses
                                               _____

estimates of
   business license cost   _____

   rental space   _____

   telephone   _____

   answering machine   _____

   answering service   _____

   credit line with local bank   _____

   legal and/or accounting fees _____

   secretarial/word processing fees and services   _____

A Marketing Program

who are your prospective clients?   _____

where are they located?   _____

who are the key persons to contact? _____

how will you present your services to them? _____

I Need:	**Comments:**
price list	_____
fees	_____
terms of payment	_____
letters of agreement or contracts	_____

Description of Your Services

outlines and illustrations	_____
brochures	_____
press kit	_____
letters of recommendation or testimonials	_____
market research data showing increasing number of business owners and managers utilizing services of a public relations consultant	_____

Niche Marketing

Those who jumpstart their careers by practicing niche marketing present themselves as specialists in solving problems at the management level.

Kevin, 44, an unemployed general manager, jumpstarted his career by making a major change in his strategy to find a new position. "For more than two years," he said, "I've marketed myself as an experienced general manager seeking a top management position. I've made hundreds of telephone calls and mailed several thousand letters and resumes. I've had a few interviews, but no offers."

Kevin's record of poor responses mirrors that of other general managers seeking employment in the 1990s. The major reason is that top managers, senior human resource managers, and executive recruiters in the present employers market are looking for goal-directed, results-oriented, problem-solvers—candidates who can show they made major improvements in their former positions. Candidates like Kevin often attract more attention by applying niche marketing: present yourself as capable of solving specific problems at the management level, especially in your own or a related industry.

Kevin's niche program included compiling a list of companies whose products or markets he knew something about or could relate to his background. Next, he researched directories, annual reports, market research summaries, and media articles to identify companies large enough to be interested in international marketing. He then wrote each manager a personal letter that described how much he knew about the company, its products, successes, markets, and goals. The letter also summarized his experience and accomplishments in Europe and the Pacific Rim. "Marketing myself specifically and targeting key companies that understood what I had done and what I could do, paid off," Kevin said. "My 100 letters attracted 20 responses, five interviews, and two offers of employment in 90 days. Now I'm the international director of marketing for a company president who is eager for us to proceed with the expansion of their initial marketing program. Niche marketing of myself: what an improvement over searching for a general manager's role!"

If you want to sum up and market your special areas of expertise, Kevin's letter will show you one kind of format to use. The form, "Major Points to Cover" will show you the guidelines used to write Kevin's letter. You may discover that a letter marketing your specific expertise will attract more employers in the 1990s.

Kevin's Letter of Inquiry

Dear Mr. (or Ms.) Smith:

According to a recent article in *MacWeek Magazine*, Apple Europe posted $2.1 billion in revenues in 1990 and is now one of the fastest growing divisions. Apple's Japan subsidiary generated $250 million during fiscal year 1990. Market analysts expect that the installed base of Macs will reach 100,000 units by this summer.

If your company is trying to benefit from this key opportunity to expand its sales and increase profits, you will be interested in my reason for writing you this letter.

I have 20 years of experience helping major corporations introduce or expand the sales of their products and/or services in Europe, Latin America, and the Pacific Rim. I developed special tools to accomplish these objectives:

- market research programs to pinpoint potential markets and determine sales potential within new markets

- networks of international distributors in Europe, Latin America, and the Pacific Rim

Both expanded markets and improved sales emerged from carefully made plans and team efforts.

Now I am seeking a management position where I can help a major corporation introduce or expand its marketing internationally. That is my reason for writing you: my research into the activities and success of your corporation convinces me that you may be committed to the international marketplace. You may need a manager now or in the near future. If so, our meeting together may be mutually beneficial.

I will call you next week in the hope of arranging a meeting with you. You may of course call me at any time (123) 456-7890.

Very truly yours,

Name

Major Points to Cover in Letters Addressed to Niche Markets

- Write directly to the current key person (plus title) in the company or organization

- Introduce yourself

- Tell the reader what you want

- Attract the reader's interest with your experience, qualifications, results, and communications skills

- Summarize your marketable experience, interests, and goals: include specific and special knowledge, experience, current technology, and state-of-the-art skills

- Explain what you believe you can do for the reader or for the company/organization that will contribute to its growth, efficiency, reputation, and/or results

- Explain why you are interested in this particular company/organization

- Cite evidence that shows you have researched the company/organization and are convinced you want to work there

- Invite the reader to contact you by telephone, FAX, or mail

- Tell the reader you will contact him or her on or about a certain date

- Enclose a current resume that supports the statements mentioned in your letter

Jean, Connie, and Kevin jumpstarted their careers because they demonstrated imagination and problem-solving skills to their managers, peers, and customers in ways that got them their ideal job. You, too, may want to introduce new ideas, new technology, or a report to your manager. You may want to become a consultant, or you may feel that niche marketing can open doors for you that your present search for employment has failed to do. Using your imagination will help you create your ideal job.

Effective Letter Writing

Writing convincing and persuasive letters is an essential skill in today's information society. Well written letters can open doors to key people, convince individuals and institutional managers to lend money, sell millions of dollars worth of goods, move people to make major decisions, and invite responses from prospective employers and customers.

This chapter explains the techniques needed to write results-producing letters and mailing pieces. It takes you through the overall process of organizing your thoughts for maximum clarity and impact, defining your task, selecting and presenting the information you want to deliver, and telling the reader what you want and what you offer.

Getting Started: Key Points to Consider

I. Define Your Purpose for Writing
   State it clearly, concisely, and precisely. Before you write it, try to look at it from the readers' perspective: what are his or her needs and interests?

   Examples
   - introduce yourself as a person seeking assistance, information, a meeting with the reader, or a response to your letter/resume/mailing piece/brochure/or telephone call

   - describe what you want and what you offer if you are a candidate for employment

   - present yourself as a marketing representative of a product or service

   - show your ability to organize and present information likely to be of interest to the reader

   - show your concern for attracting a favorable response to your letter/mailing piece/brochure

   - explain what actions the reader can take to respond to your letter/mailing piece/brochure

   - describe what actions you plan to take to follow up your letter/mailing piece, if appropriate

   - express your appreciation for courtesies extended by the reader

II. Attract the Reader's Attention
   - Select an appropriate professional format by using an appropriate quality, size, and color of paper

III. Write Professionally and Naturally
   - sound friendly, human, positive

   - avoid jargon and buzz words

   - don't speak ''up'' or ''down'' to the reader

Six Success Stories

People often ask me to help them write letters, brochures, or mailing pieces to accomplish a special purpose. In my practice, I work with clients to (1) clearly define their purpose in writing; (2) select the most professional format to use; (3) show the reader concern for meeting his or her needs and interests; and (4) explain how the reader should respond, if appropriate.

Six clients who jumpstarted their careers to higher or more rewarding levels of work through their letters are shown below. They show you what they wanted, how they expressed it, and the success they achieved as a result of it.

Bill, 28, an inside salesperson for a sporting goods retailer, needed a letter that would show the reader—a director of human resources—his best qualifications. He hoped his letter would result in an interview for a position that he lacked experience in. Bill determined that his purpose in writing the letter was to show the reader his imagination, determination, can-do attitude, aggressiveness, and quickness. The completed letter appears below:

Dear Sir:

I am responding to your recent advertisement for a TV Time sales representative, which appeared in the Sunday edition of *TV News.*

I am now selling sporting goods for the company named on my resume. If you stop in at any time, you can form your own opinion of my ability as a salesperson. You can pretend you are interested in shopping for clothes, tennis racquets, whatever. You can personally evaluate my sales abilities and I'll have no way of identifying you. I am 6 feet tall and have blond hair.

I will be doing my job because I take pride in doing it, not merely trying to impress a prospective employer. I learned this and a previous job quickly, set and achieve my own high standards, and am always the top sales representative for any of the employers shown on my resume. I hope you will want to meet me. I already know I want to meet you.

Sincerely,

Bill F.

Bill was rated the best of the 25 candidates, and he got the job. "I learned that my attitude and imagination sometimes are more important than having the required or preferred experience, especially if an employer is willing to train an employee and develop him or her in the company," Bill said.

You, too, may need a letter that emphasizes your personality, positive attitude, determination to get an interview, and whether or not you have the employer's required or preferred experience. If you do, begin by showing your commitment to advancing your career by means of hard work, results produced to date, and concern for meeting company objectives. Include facts that show your accomplishments when working with people, with data, and/or with things related to the position for which you are applying. Emphasizing your attitudes and skills and how they can solve problems can get you the interview you want.

Jack, 32, a high school machine shop instructor, needed a letter that would help him *match* his experience with an employer's need for an assistant foreman in a local manufacturing company. Jack began by designing a list of qualifications of interest to the employer: his experience with the same equipment used by the employer, his experience teaching students of different grade levels to operate such equipment, and his interest in the company. Jack's completed letter appears below:

Dear Sir:

I am responding to your advertisement for an assistant foreman, which appeared in the *San Leandro Times* on Sunday, June 11, 1989.

Since 1981, I have been the machine shop instructor at Sonora High School in Sonora, California. I teach beginning students the basic operations of the drill press and the engine lathe. I teach advanced students taper turning and thread cutting on the lathe; they also learn to set up and operate the vertical milling machine.

My machine shop experience includes the set up and operation of engine lathes, vertical and horizontal milling machines, sensitive and radial drill presses, shapers, boring mills, vertical turret lathes, surface grinders, cylindrical grinders, and universal grinders. As a planner, I had some experience programming an N/C drill press.

I am confident that my teaching experience would be an asset when carrying out the assistant foreman's responsibilities. I believe your position would offer me the new challenge I am seeking at this time. I am also confident that I would contribute to the timely, accurate, and efficient production of your company.

Per your request for this information, my present salary is $32,600.

I look forward to hearing from you soon. Enclosed is my resume for your review.

Sincerely,

Jack C.

Jack's straightforward letter matched the employer's technical requirements. His concern for contributing to the employer's obvious need of efficiency appealed to the employer. Jack was interviewed and hired.

If you want to write a letter that requires you to match your experience and goals with an employer's requirements, begin by listing the experience that relates to what the employer needs and wants. If you don't match the employer's needs and wants, you are not likely to get an interview; be sure to emphasize work done, results produced, and skills applied, learned, or self-taught. When matching your experience to an employer's requirements, write as though you are ready and equipped to *perform* the job he or she wants done.

George, 46, a self-employed consultant, wanted to write a letter to send to 100 top managers. He wanted his letter to *summarize* his specialized and in-depth experience for major corporations. He planned to mail his letter first to top managers for whom he had previously provided consulting services.

George's summary letter appears below:

Dear Sir:

I am a packaging research and marketing specialist. Since 1975, I have been directly involved in packaging research, testing, development, investigation, and marketing of various container concepts for such corporations as the Hurtz and Diske Division, Frenco, and the Translantic Sugar Company, among others.

I am writing to request a meeting with you. I would like to discuss ways to handle problems that might arise in your packaging and shipping activities as your organization expands in the years ahead.

I can:
- Reduce excessive product damage losses wherever they occur

- Develop solutions and reduce costs when planning and using containers and packaging materials

- Improve services to significant customers

Now I am seeking a technical or general management position. Having provided consulting services for your corporation in 1973 and 1975, I am already familiar with your packaging policies and shipping activities and procedures. My enclosed resume presents details of my experience to date.

I will call you next week in the hope of arranging a meeting with you at your earliest convenience.

Very truly yours,

George S.

George's summary letter attracted 10 responses, seven interviews, and two employment offers. He accepted the most attractive offer, and is now vice-president, package research and marketing for a Fortune 500 corporation.

To market your specialized and/or technical experience to key managers in organizations that have problems you can handle, begin by summarizing your areas of expertise. Include several examples of accomplishments and the names of organizations for whom you have provided services. Be specific—describe problems confronted, steps taken, and results produced; such data demonstrates your credibility. Your summary letter is likely to be effective if you have first identified the key persons—and their titles—who might most quickly respond to your special expertise and proposal, and if you write in a language they can easily understand. Enclose your resume; it should confirm and support your letter in every detail.

Chris, 28, a community college student seeking part-time work to help pay his expenses, needed a mailing piece that he could send to local homeowners and residents. He wanted to describe the services he offered and his qualifications, and explain how he could be contacted.

Chris's postcard-sized mailer is shown on the next page. Using the geographical edition of the telephone directory, he prepared a list of 1,000 homes in his community. He mailed 100 cards per week to test the responses. He learned to screen responses to select jobs he could best handle. Soon he had enough work scheduled to keep him busy for the entire semester.

I AM A COLLEGE STUDENT SEEKING PART-
TIME WORK TO PAY MY EXPENSES. DO YOU
NEED SOMEONE TO

Paint or Spray?

☐ interiors

☐ exteriors

Repair or Renovate Buildings?

☐ roofs

☐ carports

☐ interior aluminum windows, doors, and locks

Work in the Garden?

☐ construct or repair fences

☐ plant, prune, remove trees

I have five years of experience. Bondable. Excellent
references. Call for free estimates (123) 456-7890.
                                                  Chris.

To prepare a mailing piece that will publicize your product(s) or services to potential customers, begin by describing your product or service. Ask yourself who needs it and why is your product(s) unique. Ask yourself why your potential customer(s) will benefit from it and tell them 1–5 ways your product(s) or service(s) will meet their needs. Tell your readers when and how to contact you or leave a message.

Randy, 42, a former vice-president of engineering for an internationally-known heavy equipment manufacturer, had concluded from his recent employment interviews that many top managers of American corporations are complacent, outdated, and narrow in the way they recruit engineering managers. "They tell me they're concerned about hiring candidates who can help them meet engineering specifications," he said. "Well, that's important, but in the competitive 1990s market, other factors are equally important: hiring managers who can improve the sequential process of purchasing/engineering/production/marketing/customer service. Modern managers need to dedicate themselves to improving quality control and quality assurance from the point of view of both management and the consumer."

Randy, determined to apply recent state-of-the-art ideas

and technologies to make American companies more competitive, also needs a "new age" way to prescreen top level managers to find ones who share his beliefs, dedication, and expertise.

Randy's "new age" prescreening letter appears below. In my practice, I call it a prior mutual agreement letter: the writer deliberately attempts to discover whether the interviewer shares his or her convictions about the importance of applying new ideas to existing operations. The writer, in fact, proposes the agenda and participates in the interview on an equal basis with the employer; the focus is on exchanging points of view and convictions. Many prospective and actual technical or general managers apply this format to separate progressive from nonprogressive managements in their search for employment.

Dear Sir:

I know you are concerned about your company's success in competing against both domestic and international competitors. One of the ways to compete successfully is to stay technologically ahead of your competitors. Another is to make your product or service so superior and more reliable that underpricing by competitors becomes ineffective and offers no advantage in obtaining market share.

I am seeking a position in manufacturing operations in a company whose managers are asking themselves the following questions:

- Are our customers satisfied with our product or service? How do we know?

- Are our suppliers meeting our delivery schedules with conforming material? Do we have too many suppliers?

- Do our factory managers use statistical process control (SPC) techniques to help us build it right the first time?

- Does every employee regard quality as his or her responsibility or leave it to the quality assurance department?

- Do our employees subscribe to quality being defined as "fitness for use by the customer" instead of "conformance to specifications"?

If you are seeking answers to these questions, I can help you find them.

I have more than 15 years of experience in manufacturing operations. I have successfully used SPC, PAT (product audit testing), JIT (just-in-time manufacturing), and vendor rating systems to obtain excellent results in product quality and cost improvement.

I am currently seeking a position in a company that is committed to being the leader in its industry, one that will welcome my experience and skills to make an impact on corporate profitability.

You may perceive that your company can benefit from all or a part of my expertise at this time. I will welcome an opportunity to meet with you to discuss our objectives in a way that may be mutually beneficial. The enclosed resume shows you my experience and results.

I will call you next week in the hope of arranging a meeting with you at your convenience. You may call me at (000) 123-4567 in the evenings or on weekends.

Sincerely,

Randy S.

Randy designed an employment search program; the objectives are to (1) contact managers he already knew or could meet, (2) write directly to the presidents and/or vice-presidents of medium-sized manufacturers throughout the Southwest, where he preferred to work, and (3) contact and request assistance from a select number of executive recruiters known to have served major manufacturers.

Randy's program continued during a four-month period of calling first, writing and mailing his letter and resume, and calling again. He also kept in touch with recruiters. He also followed up leads that were developed from other sources. Randy completed one personal and two telephone interviews during this period, but didn't believe any of the interviews was worth following up. Then, as so often happens, after a few weeks he received a telephone call from a director of human resources in a multinational corporation headquartered in the Southwest. From their conversation, he decided to accept an appointment for an interview. His first and subsequent meetings with the company president were a reflection of mutual recognition and regard for applying new ideas, new developments, and state-of-the-art technologies. The employment agreement and compensation package were easily worked out, and now Randy is vice-president of engineering for the company. "More important than getting the job," Randy said, "was knowing that I had staked out my position and expected prospective employers to recognize it. Luckily, the company president shares most of my beliefs. Now that I'm working for him, I'm looking forward to some good years ahead. If I hadn't taken charge of the initial interviews and spoken from my convictions, I might have ended up in just another job."

To locate a manager with whom you can apply better general or technical management ideas, developments, or technologies, begin by listing the ones you deem important for you to manage and/or apply. Describe your experience in applying them. Avoid job offers that require you to "fit into" a position that offers you little or no freedom to apply your views. Pursue all available avenues of inquiry and leads that will help you locate the "right" manager. If you seek the services of executive recruiters, first contact ones known to have had experience serving both employers and candidates for employment in your industry or in those that interest you.

Robert, 53, vice-president of new product development, wanted to write a letter to executive recruiters. He wanted help in locating a top management position in specified industries and geographical areas. If you write to executive recruiters, you must provide them with detailed information about yourself. Bear in mind that executive recruiters serve the interests of *employers* who request their help in finding employed, highly qualified, and well-educated candidates who have outstanding track records and references. If you believe you are such a candidate, contacting your own carefully selected list of executive recruiters might be worthwhile.

I provide my clients with a checklist to help them gather and present information about themselves that executive recruiters need to know. They complete the checklist and then transfer this information to the letter to executive recruiters.

Robert completed the checklist below.

My reasons for writing you now _____

My plans for the future: level of position I'd
like to find _____

Recent changes in my status _____

  promotions _____

  level of responsibility _____

  prospects for advancement _____

  accomplishments _____

Date available for referrals _____

Criteria to consider

  acceptable geographical area _____

  expanding industry _____

  progressive company/corporation _____

  preferred management style _____

  compensation package _____

Special instructions: referrals to company clients acceptable only after writer's approval _____

Best time, place, and method of contacting
the writer _____

Robert used his checklist notes to write the letter below:

Dear Sir:

I am writing to request your assistance in locating company clients who may be interested in my qualifications and accomplishments shown on the enclosed resume.

Having achieved all my goals after three years with my present employer, I am now looking for new challenges. Perhaps you may know or meet senior managers seeking a candidate with my experience.

Since 1985, I have been promoted twice by my present employer: from assistant product development manager to manager, and then to vice president of new product development. My responsibilities include:

- developing and introducing new products for sales and distributing nationally and internationally

- restructuring present product lines to increase revenue and meet changing consumer needs

- effecting day-to-day cost savings and organizational changes

- formulating and implementing new strategic directions

Now I am seeking a new challenge in a senior management position where I can continue to contribute to company growth. Presently employed, I plan to find and negotiate for a new position within the next year. Our meeting together at your convenience might be mutually beneficial. You may call me at my office during the day (000) 123-4567 or at my home in the evenings or on weekends (000) 123-4567.

Thank you in advance for your interest and assistance.

Very truly yours,

Robert F.

Robert interviewed 10 executive recruiters and concluded that five of them might be able to effectively represent him with their company clients. He learned that some executive recruiters prefer selecting up to five qualified candidates for live job openings, and he was confident that he would be one of them. Having written a letter that produced valuable responses from executive recruiters, he knew he had succeeded in taking the first step toward the challenging position he had in mind. He was willing to wait the weeks or months required to find the "ideal" position. Sure enough, his patience paid off; one of the recruiters referred him to a company president seeking a candidate who had new product development experience. Robert—one of five candidates considered—got the job. "Writing effective letters is an indispensable skill for managers in this present information age," he said. "In my letters, I presented myself as wanting to be on the "cutting edge" of new developments in a progressive company. Saying what I wanted, and saying it clearly, got me the interview that got me this job!"

To request assistance from recruiters, complete the checklist on page 112. Take your time. Enter information that shows your goals, your accomplishments, and your strengths. The result can be a letter that impresses the reader, one that convinces him or her that he or she should meet you. Results in the form of interviews and employment offers are the ones your letters can generate.

Effective Resume Writing

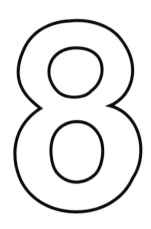

Convincing, results-oriented resumes motivate readers to open doors for you that you can't open in any other way. Such resumes present your personal qualifications and goals in ways that meet your reader's needs, interests, and values. Most resumes don't do this—many are dull, unimaginative, and do not show the writer's attractive personal qualities, special strengths, or goals. Dull resumes resemble headstones: they show beginning and ending dates, but nothing in between to inspire readers to act on the writer's behalf.

This chapter explains how you can do what successful job/career changers do: plan, organize, and write convincing and persuasive resumes that inspire readers to want to meet you. You will begin by reviewing a checklist of outstanding features in resumes known to have attracted responses, interviews, and employment offers. With those features to guide you from beginning to end, you will be able to write a resume that reports your highest and best qualifications in a clear, complete, and convincing way.

Stephen, 42, an unemployed grant and proposal writer, did not follow a checklist of his outstanding features when planning and writing his resume. His resume shows his qualifications in a poor light: lack of detailed information about his employment record, vague objectives, and—in his last line—an effort to show his sense of humor, a risky undertaking in a resume.

STEPHEN S.   123 Norcross Street
(000) 123-4567   Anytown, USA 12345

===

OBJECTIVE: Employment that is socially useful, decently remuner-
                        ative, and culturally rewarding in an environment
                        where matters of high importance are tempered with
                        humors and neckties are mandatory only in life-
                        threatening emergencies.

EXPERIENCE: Fifteen years as a grant and proposal writer for foun-
                        dations and government agencies; organizer of educa-
                        tional programs and symposia for professionals and
                        the general public.

SPECIAL   Abilities include recognizing and activating the rele-
SKILLS: vant and appropriate as distinct from BS and the bi-
                        zarre.

EDUCATION: Degrees in Philosophy and Greek

AGE: 40

PERSONAL: Unknotted by marriage but nailable

It is not surprising that he received no responses from the
100 nonprofit agency managers to whom he had sent a
copy of his resume.

Getting Started   To plan and write a resume, begin by reviewing and apply-
                           ing the five resume planning guidelines shown below.
                           Each one provides you with suggestions that can help you
                           plan and write result-producing resumes.

Resume Planning   Prepare and maintain a career journal. Begin by preparing
Guidelines   a complete, accurate, factual record of your employment
                           experience to date. Write it in the format shown below. Up-
                           date it periodically by recording descriptions of new re-
                           sponsibilities, abilities, skills, accomplishments, awards,
                           or rewards. Your career journal becomes the source from

which you prepare a resume at major turning points in your life and career.

Example:

Career Journal   **Date:**

mon./yr.–mon./yr.   *TITLE* (all caps), Company/Organization (Upper and Lower Case), city, state

Reporting to (title), describe what you do or did. Use action verbs. (See "Action Verbs" later in this chapter.)

Include summaries of:

- skills learned on the job
- self-taught skills
- skills acquired from in-house training programs
- skills learned from consultants
- abilities acquired from continuing education/training programs
- abilities acquired from a change of responsibilities, lateral, or vertical moves
- results/accomplishments/benefits that your work produced for peers/managers/customers
- reason(s) for leaving each position:

  list reasons that show you acted in your own best interests at the right time or in response to forces over which you had little or no control

Examples:

Acting in your own best interest at the right time:

- resigned to accept a higher-paying position
- resigned to accept a position offering an opportunity to learn or improve management skills
- resigned to accept a position offering an opportunity to learn or improve technical skills
- recruited to accept a new position at a higher level
- resigned to enroll in or complete an education program
- resigned to become self-employed
- resigned: no prospects for advancement

Acting in response to forces over which you had little or no control

- position eliminated

- laid off or lack of work

- company plans to relocate—declined to accept offer in the new location

- position eliminated here and transferred overseas

Emphasize your work experience during the past 10 or 15 years.

The Chronological Resume
Using Your Career Journal to Write a Resume

George, 32, a former customer service manager for a credit management company, decided to seek a top management position in the same profession. Knowing that top managers in credit management companies often have top-level openings that have not been advertised, he decided to not include an objective on his resume. Instead, he showed the skills he wanted to apply in his new position, and used his resume to negotiate an offer for a higher-paying position. He soon found and accepted a better position in another credit management company. His positive attitude, determination to market himself, and professional experience paid off. "I knew I could talk my way into a higher position if I could find one," he said. "Now I see my resume as a marketing tool for opening negotiations, not merely a report—it helped me attract management to my background and goals."

George's chronological resume appears on the following page.

GEORGE H.
(000) 123-4567

123 Sacramento Street
Anytown, USA 12345

SPECIAL SKILLS:

Work well independently or as a member of a team. Can research and handle a wide variety of administrative and clerical details, write reports, manage supervisors, and/or clerical employees.

EXPERIENCE:

1/12/84–present

Manager, Customer Service, National Management Company, Santa Rosa, California

Report directly to the manager of operations. Responsibilities include: planning, managing, and administering all phases of customer service and clerical departments. Maintain files and service agreements with 250 retailers and 42,000 revolving customer accounts. Process retail billings and approve dealer settlements up to $40,000 per month. Supervise five bookkeepers and prepare a daily journal and reconciliation report. Hire, train, and counsel 5–15 employees. Recommend raises and/or promotions for all employees in the company.

Accomplishments: Designed and applied communications procedures that reduced merchant complaints in six months. Reduced six-month backlog of clerical work. Eliminated outstanding revolving charge due business and activated turnaround to within one day.

Reason for Leaving: Company moved to Atlanta. Declined to accept management's offer of advancement to move with them. Prefer to remain in the Bay area.

EDUCATION:

Graduate, Alhambra High School, Alhambra, California.

To write a chronological resume that transfers material from your career journal into a resume that produces results, begin by reviewing the "Resume Planning Guidelines" for suggestions that will help you produce a professional resume.

Changing to a New Industry or Profession

Russell, 46, a former assistant controller for a mainframe computer manufacturer, quit to seek a controller's position in a growth-committed company outside of the volatile computer industry. "I believe my financial management experience can benefit almost any industry," he said. "but I want to show both my professional point of view and my record of results." Russell began to write his chronological resume after he had first reviewed and applied suggestions from "Resume Planning Guidelines" (pages 116–118), "Examples of Personal Qualities to Show in Your Resume" (page 123), and "Advice from Experts (page 135). To show his personal regard for results, he paid attention to listing his special accomplishments; his chronological is shown on the next page.

RUSSELL K.	123 Lime Avenue
O: (000) 123-4567	Anytown, USA 12345
H: (000) 123-4567	

OBJECTIVE: Controller for a company committed to increasing sales in national and international markets.

EXPERIENCE:

5/84–9/91   <u>Assistant Controller</u>, B.T. Lane Company, Santa Clara, California

Reporting to the chief financial officer, administered payroll, corporate disbursements, billing, advertising budgets, travel, fleet, and benefits accounting. Managed 10 managers and sixty employees. Budget responsibility up to $1.4 million.

Special Accomplishments: designed and implemented a time and attendance system utilizing box code readers (saves approximately $200,000 in supervisorial review and clerical data entry). Also defined and introduced an integrated accounts payable system which increased efficiency approximately by 30%.

3/80–1/84   <u>Manager, Accounting Services</u>, Imperial Van Services, Costa Mesa, California

Reporting to the vice president, administered payroll, cost accounting, benefits accounting. Packaged and consolidated the cost and material accounting departments. Developed accounting policies and procedures for two warehouses owned by the parent corporation. Managed three managers and nineteen employees.

Special Accomplishments: introduced and provided continuing cross-training management development programs.

7/75–9/79   <u>Manager, Cost Accounting</u>

Reporting to the assistant controller, responsibilities included writing and analysis of product costs. Developed a system for capturing labor expenditures, which saved approximately 200 man hours and provided more accurate and timely data.

Result: Promoted to manager, accounting services

EDUCATION: Bachelor of Science degree
California State University
Pasadena, California

Russell mailed 150 letters and resumes to his carefully researched list of chief executive officers in medium-sized companies. While awaiting responses from them, he registered with an agency that provides part-time financial management executives with temporary assignments. Working on short-term assignments, Russell soon learned to tell managers what he was looking for and what he was qualified to do. From a referral, Russell arranged an interview and later accepted an employment offer he couldn't afford to reject.

If you want to transfer out of one industry and into another, begin by completing your employment record in your "Career Journal." Next, after you have reviewed "Resume Planning Guidelines," "Examples of Personal Qualities to Show in Your Resume," and "Advice from Experts," write your resume to show your employment record and the outstanding personal qualities that you want to emphasize. Write about the work you have done and the results you have produced.

Examples of Personal Qualities to Show in Your Resume

Qualities   **Examples**

- motivation   _____

- courage   _____

- imagination/creativity/resourcefulness   _____

- flexibility   _____

- interest in contributing solutions to present
  and past business-related problems   _____

- ability to initiate or apply policy   _____

- effort to acquire new knowledge, tech-
  niques, or skills   _____

- success in applying new knowledge, techniques, or skills that have been acquired
  from any one or all of the following activities: self-teaching, on-the-job training, and
  academic or vocational education   _____

- promotions/commendations/awards re-
  ceived from employers/peers/community   _____

Targeting Your Experience to Reach a Special Goal

Some people want to write a chronological resume that will target their experience to get a job they've wanted for a long time.

Ron, 42, a former real estate appraiser, needed a resume that would convince readers he had long been preparing himself to qualify for the position of residential real estate appraiser in his county. First, he used his career journal to record all the facts, workshops, and licenses that his prospective employer would look for in his resume. Second, he showed his personal qualities of perseverance and accomplishments in his resume. Third, he reviewed the key verbs from the list of "Action Verbs" at the end of this chapter. Ron's chronological resume, shown on the next page, portrays him to be a factual, goal-directed, applicant whose employment record shows experience and accomplishments. As a result of his impressive resume and employment interview, the county employment officer offered the position to Ron.

To write a resume that targets your experience and goals toward achieving a special objective, begin by recording in your career journal all the details of your work experience that shows your strengths, accomplishments, and personal qualities. Select examples and data that are related to your readers' interests, and list at least five good reasons why you should be hired. If your objectives are realistic, and you are in the right place at the right time, you will increase your chances of being offered the position you really want.

Ron's resume on the next page will serve as a valuable guideline to follow. First, he lists his objectives. Second, he shows why he is qualified for the position. Third, he includes data, experience, and license that is required for employment.

RON W.   123 Burgoyne Street
(000) 123-4567   Anytown, USA 12345

OBJECTIVE: Residential real estate appraiser where I can apply
                      eight years of experience, completion of continuing ed-
                      ucation courses, and the required license to qualify for
                      this position in northern California.

CERTIFICATE: Appraiser for Property Tax Purposes (No. 3185) Issued
                      by California State Board of Equalization on June 12,
                      1988

LICENSE: Realtor Associate (14763), DRE

EXPERIENCE: Appraiser I, "x" County, southern California

                      Reported directly to the supervisor of appraisers. Con-
                      ducted on-site inspections of residential properties in
                      the county; wrote numerous summary reports of fac-
                      tors contributing to value estimates.

                      Accomplishments: Assigned to handle special on-site
                      inspections in other areas; received certificate of com-
                      mendation for productivity, positive attitude, and
                      skill in completing projects on time.

3/82–1/86   Residential Real Estate Appraiser, James O'Brien &
                      Associates, Sacramento, California

                      Assisted in appraising single-family properties; gath-
                      ered data, compiled weekly Fannie Mae URAR re-
                      ports; and acquired experience in residential real es-
                      tate cost estimating. Resigned to accept offer from "x"
                      county.

EDUCATION: Bachelor of Science degree
                      San Diego State University
                      Major: Economics. Also completed nine courses in real
                      estate appraisal. Details available on request.

Summarizing Your Experience—Briefly

Gloria, 41, a recently unemployed property manager, needed a resume that would show property managers she was "one of them." First, she entered in her career journal the words, phrases, results, and responsibilities she knew they would want to see. Next, after reviewing "Resume Planning Guidelines," "Examples of Personal Qualities to Show in Your Resume," and "Advice from Experts," she selected the format on the next page.

Gloria's factual, to-the-point entries in her resume immediately attracted return telephone calls from professional property managers. Several—having no openings—introduced her to key managers who might have openings; soon Gloria was busy scheduling first and second interviews. One month later, she accepted an offer from a leading commercial property firm with plans to expand throughout northern California. "My resume showed my readers that I was 'one of them' and knew what they were looking for when searching for applicants like me," she said. "My resume was just right."

If you want to write a resume that is brief, factual, and shows the kind and level of experience that readers in your field will look for, begin by jotting down in your career journal brief entries that describe the responsibilities you performed. Be factual, succinct, and report results. If you succeed in saying the "right" things in the way most likely to attract key persons in your field, you will have increased your prospects of attracting interest and support from prospective employers.

Gloria's resume, shown on the next page, is a guideline that will help you write your resume so that it attracts interest from readers who feel you are "one of them."

GLORIA   123 Fairfield Road
(000) 123-4567   Anytown, USA 12345

OBJECTIVE: Property manager where I can apply more than eight years of commercial property management experience for a Fortune 500 corporation.

EXPERIENCE: <u>Property Manager</u>, Marchant Corporation, Rochester, New York

1/82–7/91   Reporting directly to the president, responsibilities included:

- membership in a team that worked with architects to design space for the new company headquarters building (12 stories, 900 employees)

- arranging and overseeing social units for 400–500 employees

- planning and purchasing of all furniture and equipment

- arranging and administering all office service activities: communications, supplies, records, products, and related facilities

- negotiating and administering all office leases and subleases

1/79–11/81   <u>Marketing Representative</u>. Marketed company office products to select commercial customers on the East Coast prior to being promoted to the newly-created position of property manager in Rochester, New York.

EDUCATION: Bachelor of Science Degree
University of the Pacific
Major: Business Administration

The Functional Resume
Changing from One
Profession to Another

Some people want to write a functional resume that will help them jumpstart their career out of one profession into another.

Gordon, 38, an executive director of a large seminary in southern California, resolved to leave the "religion business" and the seminary lifestyle. After he had reviewed the guidelines and lists found in this chapter, he selected the functional resume format as the one most likely to help him market his qualifications into the for-profit community. He wanted to apply his experience in recruiting, hiring, and employee relations to the needs of a large corporation where he was willing to work in a staff or line role. First, he summarized his qualifications in his career journal, and then presented them as special skills in his functional resumes.

To write a functional resume, begin by summarizing brief descriptions of your strengths, especially ones that you want to apply or develop now. Before you proceed to write a functional resume, however, step back and evaluate the advantages and disadvantages of various resume writing formats described on page 130.

GORDON F.   123 El Pueblo Street
(000) 123-4567   Anytown, USA 12345

OBJECTIVE: A position in human resources or employee relations
                    where I can apply more than eight years of experience
                    in interviewing, hiring, training, and counseling
                    adults.

SPECIAL SKILLS

INTERVIEWING: Recruited, hired, and trained professional, technical,
                    and clerical employees for management, accounting,
                    and clerical positions.

TRAINING: Designed and developed numerous ongoing training
                    programs for 1–20 employees to improve supervisory
                    and communications skills, enhance employee motiva-
                    tion, develop leadership, and encourage cross-training
                    among clerical employees.

COUNSELING: Counseled hundreds of adults in such areas as drug
                    and alcohol abuse, vocational guidance, and marital
                    and divorce issues.

MANAGEMENT: Defined local—sometimes community—objectives;
                    planned and approved public relations policies and
                    programs; prepared and administered an annual
                    budget that increased from $50,000 to $300,000 in five
                    years.

EXPERIENCE:

4/7/82–11/2/89   Executive Director, "x" Community Center, Stockton,
                    California

                    Initiated and implemented new policies and proce-
                    dures; created new programs; and expanded staff from
                    7 to 20 employees.

EDUCATION: M.S. degree, California State University
                    Bachelor of Divinity degree, General Seminary, New
                    York, New York

Choosing the Right Format

Before you begin to write your resume, review the resume formats that are available to you. The previous examples show commonly used formats that will help you achieve your goals. Here is a list of the advantages and disadvantages of each:

The Chronological Resume

Advantages:

Shows your advancement and length of employment with each company/organization/employer. Enter periods of employment by mon./yr.–mon./yr.

Gives the prospective employer latitude in considering you for one or more positions for which you may have qualifying skills.

Enables you to easily summarize your relevant volunteer work experience.

Enables you to include your part-time experience while attending college.

Disadvantages:

Does not enable an experienced consultant to emphasize problems confronted in depth, sophisticated methods used, complex solutions provided, and benefits produced. (An attached summary of accomplishments would enable a consultant to present a complete record of experience.)

Who is it for?

Any serious job seeker/career changer

The Functional Resume

Advantages:

It is not a "resume" at all: rather, it is a structured, written "spear" thrown at one's market to locate hoped-for new openings or ones that you might fill whether or not you have the required experience.

Enables you to market your experience by function or functional titles, and the number of years in these positions.

Chronological dates of employment can be listed at end of the resume.

Disadvantages:	The reader cannot easily understand for which employer you performed the functions.
Who is it for?	Experienced executives, managers, professional workers, business office professional employees, and anyone trying to market experience by function to qualify for a job in another industry, field, or career.

Avoid Over-Generalizing

Some people never succeed in planning and writing resumes that inspire readers to want to meet them.

Paula, 27, a former "director of coordination" for a conference planning organization, wrote and mailed more than 300 functional resumes to personnel directors and public relations consultants throughout the west. She received no telephone calls or requests for interviews. Her resume, which listed numerous responsibilities, covered only a nine-month period of part-time employment. One reads her resume with wonder: how many of those responsibilities was she solely responsible for, and what results occurred? Here is an excerpt from her resume:

Director of Coordination   1985–1986

Responsibilities included:

- keeping current with leading-edge issues of concern to the financial services industry for prospective conferences

- brainstorming potential conferences and researching the market

- developing and implementing marketing strategies, including promotional materials, mailing list selection, advertising, and press releases

- compiling attendee critiques for improving future conferences

Her claimed strengths:

- effective in business and customer relations

- exposed to all facts of business: investment, finance, legal, real estate, EDP, marketing, and management

- instrumental in conversion of computer systems

Resumes that present such a general array of responsibilities are hard to believe. Likewise with her personal strengths. An experienced interviewer would thoroughly question every line in Paula's resume. Sadly, such clients often neglect to take the time to plan and write a professional resume; they neglect to focus on specific assignments or to report factual results. As a consequence, readers do not take the time to search for clarification or answers in interviews that the writer in most cases can provide in a well-written resume and cover letter.

Using Action Verbs

Write an effective resume that produces positive results requires using positive, active language. The following list of "Action Verbs" will help you describe your work experience, show results, and report accomplishments:

Action Verbs

applied	converted	delegated	edited
appraised	correlated	delivered	empathized
ascertained	conceded	documented	enforced
assigned	convened	deviated	established
assured	culminated	disbursed	estimated
accumulated	composed	drove	examined
administered	collaborated	digressed	experimented
activated	collected	discharged	extracted
accelerated	compiled	defrayed	encouraged
assisted	consolidated	discriminated	enlisted
authorized	contributed	discussed	expedited
analyzed	controlled	distributed	
acted	comprehended	decreased	facilitated
achieved	conformed	deleted	formulated
arranged	concurred	diversified	founded
augmented	concluded		forecasted
alleviated	conferred	earned	furnished
asserted	circumvented	effected	fabricated
advocated	contrived	engineered	facilitated
assimilated	confronted	established	filed
accrued	calculated	executed	financed
allocated	chartered	expanded	fixed
assigned	checked	experienced	followed
accommodated	classified	eliminated	
anticipated	coached	equipped	governed
adhered	communicated	evaluated	generated
ascertained	compared	encroached	grappled
attained	completed	exonerated	germinated
audited	computed	enacted	guided
approved	copied	excited	gathered
advised	counseled	equated	gave
addressed	created	enumerated	got
adapted		evolved	
adopted	directed	elicited	headed
adjusted	developed	emulated	harmonized
	demonstrated	excelled	handled
budgeted	designed	entrusted	headed
built	determined	expanded	helped
brought	detailed	embellished	
	devised	enriched	identified
coordinated	discovered	enhanced	illustrated
conducted	deferred	elucidated	imagined
conceived	dealt	endeavored	improved
constructed	detected	exerted	implemented
consulted	decided	exemplified	increased
controlled	defined	expounded	innovated

initiated
inspired
installed
integrated
interviewed
invented
improvised
indexed
initiated
informed
issued
instructed
inventoried
investigated
inspired
installed
integrated
interviewed
invented
instituted
invalidated
intensified
implicated
isolated
implied
introduced
incurred
induced
inaugurated
instigated
identified
illustrated
imagined
improvised
indexed
initiated
inspected
interpreted

justified
judged

kept
keynoted
keyworded

led
lowered

learned
lectured
listed
listened
logged

managed
maintained
mediated
manipulated
memorized
modeled
motivated
made
multiplied
memorized
mentored
met

notified
negotiated

operated
observed
obtained
offered
ordered
organized
originated

perfected
performed
pioneered
planned
prepared
progressed
promoted
paved
presented
programmed
provided
persisted
persuaded
practiced
predicated
prepared
produced
provided

projected
paved
published
perpetuated
presided
precluded
procured
presided
perceived
precipitated
prevented

queried
questioned

received
reorganized
recommended
researched
reevaluated
released
renegotiated
reported
revised
rejected
recommended
reduced
responded
represented
reviewed
regulated
retarded
restricted
restrained
reconciled
remunerated
rendered
reproduced
reinforced
replenished
reciprocated
rationalized
reasoned
recorded
summarized
simplified
solved
staffed

secured
serviced
signed
standardized
structured
submitted
supplied
surveyed
streamlined
stabilized
succeeded
strengthened
specified
supervised
selected
substantiated
sponsored
surpassed
stimulated
simulated
shaped
scheduled
schemed
screened
spoke
specialized
strategized
studied
surveyed

taught
trained
trebled
theorized
translated
transformed
typed

unified
updated
utilized

verified
validated
vindicated

wrought
wrote

Resume Writing: Advice from Experts

1. There are no hard-and fast rules governing specific style and content.

2. You will probably need at least one kind of resume format if you are searching for employment that requires you to contact strangers or enlist the help of others in your search for another job or change in career direction.

3. First write a chronological resume; the source material used to develop it becomes the material from which you can select entries for your functional resume—if you write a functional resume at all.

4. Keep in mind that employers will discount 15 to 20 percent of what you report or claim in your resume.

5. You may be hired by a peer, friend, associate, former employer, or stranger without any of them ever asking to see your resume.

6. A resume format that works well for one person—as an accurate indicator of the writer's ability to do or learn to do a particular job—may be totally wrong for another person.

7. Employers place people in functional, specialized positions. You are more likely to be hired or promoted if you show your interest in a particular position, department, project, or role.

8. Often the success of your resume mailing campaign depends on forces or factors over which you have little or no control. This may include the reader's mood, understanding, and appreciation of your background and experience; changing company needs; interests and financial standing; priorities; kinds and levels of openings; and hiring policies and priorities, among others.

9. Your resume may be rejected many times; it is part of the job search/career change process. You may never know the reasons yours was rejected. Don't take the rejections too seriously.

10. Avoid designing and writing a resume only for mass production and mailing to any and all employers; it is more productive if you invest more time in selecting a small number of employers or key representatives to contact and revise your resume to meet their known or anticipated needs.

Know the Right Time to Make Job or Career Changes

There is a right time, a not-so-right time, and a wrong time to plan and carry out major life or career changes. Often you know that now is the right time for you after you have become clear about (1) the personal changes you want to make; (2) why you want to make them now; (3) when you want to make them; (4) the kind of work you want to pursue or create; (5) the kind of lifestyle you want; and (6) whether you are willing and able to make those changes.

For example, you may want to pursue a higher position in your own field; pursue new challenges in another field; transfer into a more stable, progressive, even faster-growing company or industry; move to another part of the country (or overseas); or become self-employed to improve your financial status, among others. Once you have your goals in mind, you'll find it easier to identify and complete the steps you need to take, and you'll know when the time is right for change.

The purpose of this chapter is to help you plan and execute a major life and career change at the right time. To do so, you will prepare a written strategy for achieving maximum satisfactions and rewards from your work.

"Now" May Be the Right Time to Change

Richard, 41, a former controller for a heavy-equipment manufacturer, recognized that "now" is the right time for him to begin his search for another top financial management position with a more challenging company. "Having been the controller for my present employer for eight years," he said, "I've accomplished everything I had set out to do: for example, our sales have increased to $900 million annually, employees to 2,800 from 1,200, and the company has extended to 35 locations nationwide. I have completed a stage in my life—now is the time for me to move on. If I remain here, I'd be merely an administrator."

With the help of an Employment Search Program, Richard was able to identify and pursue realistic targets until he succeeded in attracting an offer. After six months of applying his program, he accepted a position as vice-president of finance for a computer peripheral equipment manufacturer.

If "now" is the right time for you to make major changes in your life and work, be sure you understand *why*. Compare your reasons with those of others who also made major changes. (See "10 Good Reasons" below.) Your responses will give you more self-confidence; they may also help you identify more worthwhile objectives to pursue.

10 Good Reasons for Jumpstarting Your Job/Career

Reasons	Important to me NOW	
	Yes	No

1. A competitor is experimenting with new ideas and accomplishing exciting goals. I want to learn more about employment opportunities with that company. _____ _____

2. My salary and/or compensation package have peaked with my present employer. Now is the time for me to seek a better-paying position elsewhere. _____ _____

3. Our company is cutting back on defense contracts. Now is the time for me to find a position with a more stable company that has a progressive management style. _____ _____

4. I want to work for company "x"; it is known to be the leader in our industry. _____ _____

5. I know many people, including former employees, who now work for company "y." They speak highly of the managers and their commitment to growth, including opportunities for women in management. _____ _____

6. I want a technical or general management position, or, a position leading to management in a medium-sized or small company—that's where the opportunities are in the 1990s. _____ _____

7. I feel I should enroll in and complete a formal education and/or training program that will help me advance in my present field or prepare me to enter into another job or career. _____ _____

8. I no longer want to work for a company concerned only about business and profit. I want to work for a company that is doing something socially significant and good for the environment. _____ _____

9. I want to work for a company where I can advance fast and be paid for my performance, not because I fit in and am willing to wait for management to do something for me. _____ _____

10. I want to work in a company where I can develop my expertise in management, financial services, technical engineering, manufacturing, and production. _____ _____

11. Other(s)_____

TOTAL: _____ _____

If you answer "yes" to 60% of the reasons listed, you are correct in concluding that "now" is the right time for you to make major changes in your life and work. All you will need is a plan—unless you already have your own—and the appropriate methods for "building a bridge" to your next objective.

"Now" May Be the Right time to **Prepare** *to Change*

Deborah, 34, a former marketing representative for a temporary agency, concluded that she had advanced to the highest position possible with her present employer. Deborah began wondering what lay ahead for her. One day, she said, "I'm tired of making repeat personal and telephone calls to prospective clients, and telling them we can provide the best qualified temporary workers. Truth is, we can't always provide better workers. Our company is no different from any other temporary agency. Sometimes our workers do a good job; sometimes they don't. If they don't, I'm in trouble with the client. Who needs trouble? I'm tired of being in the middle of a complaining employer and an incompetent employee."

For people like Deborah, who have concluded that they want to get out of their present job or career, now is the time for them to *prepare* for a change. Deciding to get out of a job/career and/or industry is only the first step. The second step is to define what you want to be or do, and the third step is to transfer into it, or, after completing a period of *preparation*, enter into it. Your present job now assumes a new meaning: it becomes a stable springboard from which you will embark on an educational or training program that will prepare you to qualify for a desired position or industry.

Deborah remained in her present job to maintain her steady income while she prepared to embark on a different career. "I want to become a residential real estate broker," she said. "I'll begin by completing the real estate salesperson's license requirements. Next, I'll find a broker who will let me work while I learn to make a living selling residential real estate." Deborah's plan to prepare herself to jumpstart her career allowed her to leave the temporary agency industry and begin work as a real estate salesperson without any interruption in her income.

Completing the form, "My Plan for Jumpstarting My Job or Career," will help you to determine if "now" is the time to *make* major changes or to *prepare* to make them.

My Plan for Jumpstarting My Job or Career

Reasons	Important to me NOW	
	Yes	No

1. I first need to complete an education or training program to earn a degree/license/credential/certificate required for entry or transfer into the field or job I want.

2. I should remain employed with my present employer until I receive a promised salary increase or bonus: either one will help me finance the education or training program.

3. Even though I dislike and want to get out of my present job, I can still work from 9 to 5 and have free time in the evenings or on weekends to attend classes.

4. I believe I should remain employed with my present employer until I am vested in the company retirement plan.

5. I believe I should remain employed with my present employer because the company pays all expenses for completion of work-related educational or training programs.

6. I believe I should remain employed with my present employer so I can take time off to interview key people or prospective employers and learn more about what is available for a person with my qualifications.

7. I believe I should first obtain professional advice and assistance from a career consultant, attorney, or tax attorney.

8. I believe I should first do some research and learn more about where opportunities exist in the present restructuring of the economy.

9. I believe I should first take all my vacation time I've earned before I begin to look for another position or resign from the company.

10. I believe I should first complete continuing education courses to improve my supervisory and/or management skills (communication, supervision, personnel management, computer, etc.)

11. Other(s)_____

_____

TOTAL:

If you answer "yes" to 60% of the reasons listed, you are correct in concluding that "now" is the right time to *prepare* yourself to jumpstart your job and/or career. All you will need is information about how to prepare yourself to enter into another job or career—unless you already have your own—and the appropriate methods for "building and crossing a bridge" to your next objective.

"Now" May Be a Not-So-Right Time for You to Make Major Changes

If you are employed by a company involved in a major restructuring, downsizing, merger, acquisition, or bankruptcy, you know that all of these situations can be complicated, time-consuming, and traumatic. They can affect the entire organization or only parts, departments, or branches of it. Changes occur immediately, gradually, predictably, unpredictably, or not at all. In some instances, management can decide to combine two or more functions/departments/processes, reduce resources available to handle the work, and expect more work from the employees involved.

For some employees, especially the high-salaried, long-time employed who have special skills required in that company, now may be a *not-so-right* time to resign or make major changes. In fact, now may be a special time to design and apply your own "Proactive Career Change Plan" to accomplish one or both of the following objectives: (1) remain employed; watch events unfold; look for unexpected changes and new opportunities; and, if appropriate, pursue new openings with the company; and/or (2) if you believe that your job security and advancement prospects are disappearing, you can redirect your efforts and begin your search for employment elsewhere. Whether you are pursuing (1) or (2), even (1) and (2) at the same time, you are maintaining control over your life and career choices.

Jeff, 38, a former assistant warehouse manager for a major "after market" automobile parts manufacturer, decided to apply his "Proactive Career Change Plan" while continuing to work for his present employer. "My plan enabled me to act positively on a day-to-day basis while I watched the new management's plan unfold," he said. "They wanted to hire new employees or transfer employees from corporate headquarters to the new, out-of-state owner. Within sixty days, I realized that I was not scheduled to be a part of the emerging management team, so I shifted gears. I began to search for other employment and maintain my income with a minimum loss of time, money, and morale. Good thing I pursued a new job—I jumpstarted my career into the position of warehouse manager for five warehouses at a company located a few blocks from my home."

Jeff's "Proactive Career Change Plan" appears below:

My Objectives	**Notes to Myself**
1. I remained calm, watched new policies and procedures unfold, kept a positive attitude, reminded myself that just because our company has been restructured/merged/downsized, it does not necessarily mean that my job will disappear or that I will be laid off.	
2. I developed a list of skills required to do my job, the job next to mine, and the job above me. I periodically graded myself on my competence doing each of them.	
3. I kept dated records of all communications with my manager and the personnel director regarding my performance evaluations, promised or implied salary reviews and increases, and bonuses or promotions. I responded factually, in writing, to my manager's remarks on my performance evaluations if I didn't agree with them. I signed performance evaluations by writing "I look forward to progressing with the company" to show my positive attitude and continuing interest in remaining an employee.	
4. I compiled and updated a list of the many employees who resigned or were laid off or fired. I called them to find out where they were now working. I helped them with good references when I could, and I asked them if they would help me learn about openings in the organization where they are now employed. All of them have agreed to help me.	
5. I memorized top management's personnel policies regarding layoffs, references, previous court actions, and present litigation in process.	
6. I updated my resume to show present and new responsibilities, state-of-the-art knowledge, abilities and skills, and supervisory and management experience.	

If you need a plan that will help you take charge of your career choices during restructuring, etc., begin by listing actions that will help you maintain a positive attitude and remain open to new opportunities. Be prepared, however, to redirect your energies and goals outside of your organization if needed. In the 1990s, working adults who have such a plan are more likely to execute constructive changes with less loss of time, energy, income, and morale.

"Now" May Be the Time for Research and Adventure

Tim, 35, decided he was burned out from counseling adults having trouble with alcohol abuse. "I want to escape from providing one-to-one counseling to people in trouble," he said. "But I have no idea about other kinds of work that I want to do or could do."

Like Tim, you will progress much faster in your search for an acceptable job or career if you keep applying the following basic guidelines:

Guidelines

1. You must *want something* from your alternative work and/or lifestyle that you are not now getting, perhaps something new, more rewarding, or more exciting.

2. You must *commit yourself* to seriously explore options of all kinds that seem to offer you prospects of giving you what you want. The options must appear realistic and possible for you to achieve at an acceptable cost now or in the near future.

3. You must *believe* that the options you choose—whether a position or a period of preparation—will give you the new satisfactions and rewards you are seeking. (Many adults have goals, even have ways to achieve them, but lack the faith that their efforts will lead to success.)

4. You must *have, acquire,* or *invent* a practical and tangible plan for achieving your objectives, and you must persist in applying your plan until you succeed.

Questions to Ask Myself

What do I want that will meet my needs?

_____

_____

What options do I wish to explore?

_____

_____

_____

Do I believe that the options I am pursuing will produce the satisfactions I want? If so, why? _____

_____

_____

My plan includes completing the following steps: _____

_____

_____

Tim kept the four basic guidelines in mind—even used them to evaluate each option he explored—during the weeks devoted to investigating alternative jobs or careers. Of each option, he would begin by asking himself, "Why not me?" Additional information, such as the cost and time required to transfer into the job or career dampened his enthusiasm. But he began to see he was making progress. One day, he wrote in his guidelines: "Of three conclusions I am becoming certain: I no longer want to sit at a desk all day; I do want to do some kind of work outdoors at least part of the time; and my wife, Diane, and I might want to join forces and operate some kind of a small business." Such conclusions help to let go of the past and begin to shape the future.

To embark on a research and adventure program, apply your own "Proactive Career Change Plan" and follow the four basic guidelines. Write down your honest feelings about the conditions you want to change and any aspirations you have about your future job or career and why it will be better. The "Prospect Criteria Summary" on the next page provides a structure of useful information. Use it to compile valuable information and insights, and decide if you want to pursue or ignore the profile of information. You may find the summary useful in evaluating options.

Prospect Criteria Summary

Worth pursuing:

1. Kind and level of work

   _____

2. Reasons it interests me now

   _____

   • personal

   _____

   • social

   _____

   • financial

   _____

   • spiritual

   _____

   • other(s)

   _____

3. Industry or profession

   _____

   • purpose

   _____

   • expanding

   _____

   • shrinking

   _____

   • new

   _____

   • established

   _____

4. Company or organization

   _____

   • headquartered where?

   _____

   • reputation in its industry

   _____

   • reputation in the community

   _____

   • size

   _____

      number of employees

   _____

      annual sales volume

   _____

5. Geographical location

   _____

      acceptable

   _____

      acceptable round-trip daily commute

   _____

6. Among people who recognize and respect
   your talents, strengths, goals, reasons for
   working there, and you theirs

   _____

   _____

   _____

7. For the right personal and professional rewards

   _____

   _____

After weeks of applying their "Proactive Career Change Plan," following the four basic guidelines, and matching acquired information against the "Prospect Criteria Summary," Tim and Diane discovered a new and adventurous goal. They found an advertisement that read: "For Sale: 50-acre Russian River lakefront property in Northern California. 25 cabins to rent, 75 canoes and rowboats, 1,500 foot waterfront, small restaurant. Call ( ) for information." They purchased the property. Now, Tim works outdoors and maintains the property, while Diane manages the business, and together they cook breakfast for visitors and service campers from all over.

"Now" May Never Be the Right Time

Some people may never be ready for research and adventure or a new job or career.

Jeannette, 31, a former accounts payable supervisor, may never be ready to undertake the necessary research, openness to adventure, and pursuit of career goals to find a more satisfying and rewarding job. "I was doing clerical and receptionist jobs when I started two years ago," she said. "When the accountant quit, the office manager asked me if I could handle the billing. I learned the billing, then taught myself to handle the payables, and even posted the books up to general ledger before I quit. I've never had or wanted to get any training in accounting. I have a B.A. degree in mathematics, but I've never used it—I've given up going after a master's degree in mathematics. I'd sure like to make more money, but I want to work only a 9 to 5 job, and I don't want to attend classes at nights or on weekends."

Talented, well-educated people like Jeannette often prefer to maintain their routines with minimal investment of time and energy into a plan that will help them qualify for better-paying positions. Often they drift from one modest-paying position to another. They neglect to focus on and pursue high-level positions that would require evidence of interest in self-improvement and ambition. Sadly, such clients often continue to accept jobs given them. As a result, their employers soon recognize their minimal ambition and give them minimal responsibilities with few opportunities for advancement.

Take Charge of the Rest of Your Life

10

You now have the tools to revitalize and jumpstart your job or career and proceed to new heights. Your challenge is to use these tools to continually update and apply your job/career strategies to meet your changing needs, to pursue new interests, and to act on new values. This chapter explains how to take charge of the rest of your life, stay on top of what's happening within and around you, and push on to success every step of the way.

Using Your Career Tools

In my practice, I help each client design and later update a "Reassessment Schedule." Each client then periodically records not only changes in his or her needs, interests, and values, but also in plans to remain current in his or her field, industry, or profession. Each one accepts personal responsibility for learning, and, if appropriate, for applying new ideas, developments, and/or technologies that will enable him or her to remain aware of prospects for career advancement and to pursue new opportunities.

A standard "Reassessment Schedule" is shown on the next page. It emphasizes knowledge, strategies, and tools that working adults will need to know, practice, and apply if they are to remain competitive in the years ahead. You, too, can use it. Enter topics, ideas, developments, technologies, and special skills that are important to you now and important to key persons in your own field, industry, or profession. Write notes to yourself in your schedule.

"Reassessment Schedule"

Topics   **Notes to Myself**

1. My changing needs, interests, and values in relation to my work include the following:

   _____

2. My recent accomplishments include:

   _____

3. My new strengths and skills include:

   _____

4. Supervisory Skills

   I plan to:

   ___ learn to be a supervisor

   _____

   ___ improve my supervisory skills

   _____

   ___ teach supervisory skills

   _____

   ___ avoid becoming a supervisor

   _____

   ___ escape from my present role as a supervisor

   _____

5. Political Skills

   ___ I enjoy participating in political activities and pursuing political objectives.

   _____

   ___ I enjoy pursuing political power and exercising it in relation to my work.

   _____

   ___ I am not very good at playing political games in the office and have no interest in improving my role or interest in this area.

   _____

   ___ I don't like political games at all and I plan to find a position where I don't need to be involved in them.

   _____

6. Communications Skills

   I want to learn or improve my skills in:

   ___ writing

   _____

   ___ speaking

   _____

   ___ chairing meetings

   _____

   ___ conducting training sessions

   _____

   ___ leading workshops/seminars

   _____

Topics   **Notes to Myself**

7. Leadership Skills

   I want to learn or improve my skills in:

   __ exercising leadership   _____

   __ leading coworkers   _____

   __ teaching others to use them   _____

8. Continuing Education

   I want to:

   __ complete a two-year degree   _____

   __ complete a four-year degree   _____

   __ complete an MA or MBA program   _____

   __ complete a training program that will
      qualify me for a license/credential/ap-
      prenticeship   _____

   __ complete courses that will help me
      advance my career and improve my
      salary   _____

9. I want to expand my "inner circle" list of
   people I already know who can be
   sources of information, support, advice,
   introductions, and/or referrals to job
   openings, opportunities, or key people
   when and if I need them. I will include
   the following names, titles, and telephone numbers: _____

10. I want to expand my "outer circle" of
    people I don't know, would like to meet,
    who can be sources of support, informa-
    tion, advice, introductions, and/or refer-
    rals to job openings, opportunities, or
    key people when and if I need them. I will
    include the following names, titles, and
    telephone numbers: _____

I need to research and locate the following facts, information, and developments that will help
me upgrade my knowledge, abilities, and skills:

_____

_____

Recognizing the Reasons for Making Changes

I often meet clients who have good, even important, reasons for making major changes in their life and work, yet they don't make them. They lack a sense of urgency to make those changes. They remain in their present job or career even though dissatisfied, and may not make any major changes at all.

Mary Lou, 35, a word processing specialist for a large law firm, had a good and important—but not a compelling—reason for making major changes in her life and work. She lacked the resolution and goalsetting skills needed to jumpstart her career in another direction. "At one time, when word processing was new, I was special," she said. "Now I am like everyone else. All the lawyers here have word processors. I feel like a second-class citizen. I want to work with people—maybe I'll be an events planner. Wonder how much money they make? But I'm too conservative to make any major changes in my life and work. Maybe someday I'll do something."

George, 48, a senior attorney and corporate counsel for a major manufacturer, also has a good and important—but not a compelling—reason for making major changes in his life and work. Indecisive, he may decide to do nothing, which is, of course, a decision. "I'm going through a parting of the ways with my employer," he said. "What's next for me—I don't know. I want no part of working for a major law firm: too much politics. Besides, I don't have the portfolio they want. I'd like to be a small town lawyer, but I wouldn't make much money. One thing I'm sure of: I need lots of variety and responsibility. How do I go about deciding what I should do next?"

Neither Mary Lou nor George is likely to make major changes until he or she feels a sense of urgency—a compelling reason—for directing his or her energies, talents, and skills toward defining and pursuing new objectives in life and work.

If you have a good and important reason for making major changes that could jumpstart your job or career, and you don't make those changes, you might end up working for someone who once had good and important reasons and *did* make them. And that person might even have achieved a higher level of satisfaction, status, and income than you!

I also meet clients who have compelling reasons for making major changes, and making them right now. Recognizing the differences between *good and important* and *compelling*, and pursuing an appropriate course of action in response to them, often marks the difference between feeling self-confident and successful or not. A compelling reason for one person, however, is not necessarily a compelling reason for another. Only you can decide whether your reasons are good and important or compelling.

If you hesitate when separating good and important from compelling reasons for making major changes in your life and work, the exercise below will help you distinguish between them. Some of my clients have selected the reasons below as ones that either compelled them to make major decisions now or that will compel them to make major decisions in the future. Check the ones that you believe are compelling reasons why you should act now or in the near future. If you've checked "yes" to six or more of the reasons below, now may be the time for you to begin making plans to jumpstart your life and career.

Examples of Compelling Reasons

	Yes	No

1. I "see the handwriting on the wall" (layoffs or resignations have occurred in your group, project, or department, and more layoffs are scheduled). _____ _____

2. I am overworked and in poor health and see no relief from the extensive pressure, demands, and overtime made on me. _____ _____

3. My boss didn't give me a promised salary increase and/or promotion, and he won't talk about it. Other employees received their promised salary increases. _____ _____

4. I'm afraid that my job—like others in the company—will be transferred elsewhere, perhaps overseas. No other suitable positions exist for me with my present employer. _____ _____

5. My boss is cruel, vindictive, and domineering. He never forgets anyone who doesn't support him, and he likes to humiliate people in meetings. I can no longer tolerate him or her. _____ _____

6. I'm tired of my job, and there's no place to transfer to with my present employer. _____ _____

7. I do not have enough formal education to qualify for the level of work I want to do, and I could complete the required education or training in a short time if I resigned and completed my formal education or training. _____ _____

8. I see new ideas, developments, and technologies bursting out all over in my industry or profession. I have all the skills and experience required to advance my career, but not in this company. _____ _____

9. I need to find a job that pays more money. I'm falling behind financially every day I work here. _____ _____

10. I've received a better-paying offer from another company if I agree to start to work there immediately. _____ _____

TOTAL: _____ _____

Recognizing the Reasons for Not Making Changes

Some of my clients confront an array of alternative options, yet they decide to remain with their present employer. For example, some know they can (1) remain in their present position, perform as well as they always have, and wait for in-company changes that may open doors to new opportunities; (2) accept their employer's offer of a lower-paying lateral transfer or be laid off; (3) accept their employer's one-time-only generous reduction-in-force separation agreement or the likelihood of later being laid off without it; or (4) accept their employer's "golden hand-shake" compensation package and layoff, including extended outplacement services. Even so, they decide to remain with their present employer, often accepting the offer of a lower-paying lateral transfer. Such clients conclude that they have a good and important, even compelling, reason for remaining with their present employer: to retain a stable—albeit lower—income so they can achieve their long-term objective of retiring at the right time. For such clients, jumpstarting their career means to make the best use of available options.

Michael, 68, a manager of civil and construction engineers for an international engineering corporation, decided to remain with his present employer but in a lower-paying position.

"At my age," he said, "I doubt any other engineering corporation of any size would hire me or could afford me. I'm too out-of-date to be hired as an engineer. So, I've decided to accept the company's offer of a lower paying position near San Francisco. At least, I'll maintain a steady, if lower, salary. Besides, in two more years, I'll be able to retire with full benefits from the company."

Knowing when you are well off, and accepting your present position as the best of possible alternatives, is another way of jumpstarting your career by accepting the best of several available alternatives. Only you can decide whether jumpstarting your career can best be done by remaining with your present employer or seeking employment elsewhere.

I often meet people who perform satisfactorily in their present jobs but don't energetically select, talk about, or pursue special work-related goals that will increase their status, position, or income. They seem to do their work and go home. Some admit to having drifted into, or were assigned to, or inherited, their present jobs. They seldom stand out among their coworkers as being ambitious, and managers do not seriously consider them for promotions. Sadly, such employees become known as satisfactory performers but not candidates for career advancement. Some of these clients drift from one job to another.

Pat, 32, an office clerk for an insurance company, has not taken charge of the rest of her life; in fact, she accepts whatever work her employer gives her. "I have a few months of inventory control experience, some in billing and accounts receivable, and four months in information systems," she said. "My resume shows me as having a little of this, a little of that, but not much in-depth experience in anything but general office work. Insurance jobs, such as claims underwriting, or claims adjusting, don't interest me at all. Oh, I've looked for other jobs, but interviewers are turned off by all of my general experience—there is no goal they can detect. Someday I'll select a goal and go after it."

Doing It Your Way

There is no "one sure way" to jumpstart a stalled career that works equally well for everyone—there are many ways. What works well for one person may not work well for another. Professional strategies and forms, such as the ones in this book, are known to be helpful for thousands of adults entering or transferring into a new job or career. Each person has, or can learn to apply, his or her own way of planning and carrying out a change from one job or career to another. Trust your instincts and intuition and applying your own common sense may reveal unsuspected talents and strengths as you pursue or create another position for yourself. Doing things in your own way, combined with the use of any or all of the ideas, strategies, and forms in this book, practically ensures your success in jumpstarting your job or career.

Harry, 28, a former truck driver for an auto parts distributor, got the job he wanted by going after it in his own way. He pursued a position as a brakeman for the Southern Pacific Railroad for more than a year. Harry completed employment applications and delivered his resume, and soon discovered that applying for the position was one thing, being hired another. So, trusting his instincts, he visited the personnel office of the Southern Pacific Railroad each week for more than a year. Soon he was on a first-name basis with the key managers in the personnel department. His perseverance paid off—nearly a year later, the company managers announced an opening for a brakeman. Because Harry was well known by this time, the personnel department offered him the position. Now a brakeman with the Southern Pacific Railroad, Harry rides the company's rails nationwide. Few job seekers would have persevered in this quest for the position they wanted. "I got my job by persevering in my efforts to get it. I knew I would have to get it my way, and I did," he said.

Mark, 49, an unemployed credit manager, also got his new job in his own way. He discovered that mailing hundreds of letters and resumes and *telling* and *showing* prospective employers—in writing—what he wanted and offered, was not attracting responses or producing interviews. Mark also concluded that without meeting and talking with the right people, he would not attract interest in his qualifications. Acting in his own way, Mark decided to walk into the first company door that could use his services. He began by reviewing the job list that he often found at the reception desk. Then he would ask to see the manager of the credit management department or the human resources director—sometimes he got an immediate interview, sometimes not.

Mark's new strategy began to produce results. One day he passed a new five-story building under construction on the corner near his home. On the site he saw the construction superintendent's sign that read "Future Home of the "X" Health Club." He knew the company would soon have credit management problems, so he asked the construction superintendent for the name of the health club's president. He called the president who told him, "I like your attitude. Few people would have walked around on that site and tracked down the superintendent." So, the president and Mark met several times, and Mark was right: He got the job offer he wanted."I knew I could get the job I wanted if I could speak for myself—not only on paper in resumes or in letters," Mark said. "So, I got my new job. But I had to do it my way."

Sylvia, 36, a psychotherapist specializing in eating disorders, concluded that merely *telling* people about her work did not attract many clients. A former model, accustomed to marketing herself on TV, Sylvia decided to present herself in a photo as part of a two-color brochure to offer readers a model that they could see and strive to imitate. As a result, her brochure both *told* and *showed* prospective clients the benefits her services could provide. "Showing myself in a picture as a 'product' of my own services attracted more clients than I had attracted during the past three months," she said. "I knew my business had a marketing problem, and I solved it. But I did it my way."

Harry, Mark, and Sylvia succeeded in jumpstarting their careers by following their instincts and intuition, and by applying the ideas, strategies, and forms in this book.

Some Clients Ask Me How They Will Know When Their Plan To Jumpstart Their Career Is Working

You will know when your plan to jumpstart your career is working when you begin to experience positive results from your efforts to:

- define and ask for what you want from other people, and feel comfortable acknowledging other people for any assistance they may have given you;

- present your marketable assets and goals to key persons, some of whom may be prospective employers;

- negotiate in a win-win way for greater responsibilities/rewards/or a better position with your present or another employer, or into a form of self-employment;

- develop and apply your own plan to identify suitable career options and get or create the job or career you want; and

- share your sense of humor with others.

You, too, may now want to jumpstart your job or career. If so, begin by imagining what you would be doing in that "better" job or career. Describe the environment in which you would be doing that "better" job or career. Describe what you would need to know or do to accept or create work in that environment. Describe the knowledge, experience, skills, education, and accomplishments you now have that would qualify you for employment in that job or career. Describe what steps you could take that would qualify you for that "better" job or career. Design and apply a plan to search for the job or career you want. Keep accurate and updated records of your progress. Acting in your own way, aided by the professional ideas, strategies, forms, and stories in this book, you, too can jumpstart your job or career into the position and opportunity you had not previously thought possible.

Appendix: Sources of Additional Information

Books

A *Question of Values* (Six Ways We Make the Personal Choices that Shape Our Lives) Hunter Lewis. New York, New York: Harper and Row, 1990.

Contact (The First Four Minutes). Leonard Zunin, M.D., with Natalie Zunin. New York, New York: Ballantine Books, 1972.

Gaining Control (Your Key to Freedom and Success). Robert E. Bennett with Kurt Hanks and Gerreld L. Pulsiplar. Salt Lake City, Utah: Franklin International Institute, Inc., 1987.

Going Home. Robert A. Raines. San Francisco, California: Harper and Row, 1979.

Leadership Is an Art. Max DePhree. East Lansing, Michigan: Michigan State University Press, 1987.

Legal Guide for Starting and Running a Small Business. Fred S. Steingold. Berkeley, California: Nolo Press, 1992.

Life Together. Dietrich Bonhoeffer. San Francisco, California: Harper and Row, 1954.

Lincoln on Leadership. Donald T. Phillips. New York, New York: Warner Books, 1992.

The Electronic Sweatshop (How Computers Are Transforming the Office of the Future and the Factory of the Past). Barbara Garson. New York, New York: Simon and Schuster, 1988.

The Seven Habits of Highly Successful People (Powerful Lessons in Personal Change). Stephen R. Covey. New York, New York: Simon and Schuster, 1985.

The Work of Nations (Preparing Ourselves for 21st Century Capitalism). Robert B. Reich. New York, New York: Alfred A. Knopf, 1991.

When Giants Learn to Dance. Rosabeth Mose Kanter. New York, New York: Simon and Schuster, 1989.

You Just Don't Understand. Deborah Tannen, Ph.D., New York, New York: Ballantine Books, 1990.